DATE DUE

			PRINTED IN U.S.A.

APR 1 9 2013

LANGUAGE AND LITERACY SERIES

Dorothy S. Strickland, FOUNDING EDITOR
Celia Genishi and Donna E. Alvermann, SERIES EDITORS

ADVISORY BOARD: Richard Allington, Kathryn Au, Bernice Cullinan, Colette Daiute, Anne Haas Dyson,
Carole Edelsky, Shirley Brice Heath, Connie Juel, Susan Lytle, Timothy Shanahan

(Continued)

For volumes in the NCRLL Collection (edited by JoBeth Allen and Donna E. Alvermann) and the Practitioners Bookshelf Series
(edited by Celia Genishi and Donna E. Alvermann), please visit www.tcpress.com.

LANGUAGE AND LITERACY SERIES (*continued*)

teaching**media***literacy*.com:
A Web-Linked Guide to Resources and Activities
RICHARD BEACH

What Was It Like? Teaching History and Culture Through
Young Adult Literature
LINDA J. RICE

Once Upon a Fact: Helping Children Write Nonfiction
CAROL BRENNAN JENKINS & ALICE EARLE

Research on Composition
PETER SMAGORINSKY, ED.

Critical Literacy/Critical Teaching
CHERYL DOZIER, PETER JOHNSTON, & REBECCA ROGERS

The Vocabulary Book: Learning and Instruction
MICHAEL F. GRAVES

Building on Strength
ANA CELIA ZENTELLA, ED.

Powerful Magic
NINA MIKKELSEN

New Literacies in Action
WILLIAM KIST

Teaching English Today
BARRIE R.C. BARRELL ET AL., EDS.

Bridging the Literacy Achievement Gap, 4–12
DOROTHY S. STRICKLAND & DONNA E. ALVERMANN, EDS.

Crossing the Digital Divide
BARBARA MONROE

Out of This World: Why Literature Matters to Girls
HOLLY VIRGINIA BLACKFORD

Critical Passages
KRISTIN DOMBEK & SCOTT HERNDON

Making Race Visible
STUART GREENE & DAWN ABT-PERKINS, EDS.

The Child as Critic, Fourth Edition
GLENNA SLOAN

Room for Talk
REBEKAH FASSLER

Give Them Poetry!
GLENNA SLOAN

The Brothers and Sisters Learn to Write
ANNE HAAS DYSON

"Just Playing the Part"
CHRISTOPHER WORTHMAN

The Testing Trap
GEORGE HILLOCKS, JR.

Reading Lives
DEBORAH HICKS

Inquiry Into Meaning
EDWARD CHITTENDEN & TERRY SALINGER, WITH ANNE M. BUSSIS

"Why Don't They Learn English?"
LUCY TSE

Conversational Borderlands
BETSY RYMES

Inquiry-Based English Instruction
RICHARD BEACH & JAMIE MYERS

The Best for Our Children
MARÍA DE LA LUZ REYES & JOHN J. HALCÓN, EDS.

Language Crossings
KAREN L. OGULNICK, ED.

What Counts as Literacy?
MARGARET GALLEGO & SANDRA HOLLINGSWORTH, EDS.

Beginning Reading and Writing
DOROTHY S. STRICKLAND & LESLEY M. MORROW, EDS.

Reading for Meaning
BARBARA M. TAYLOR, MICHAEL F. GRAVES,
& PAUL VAN DEN BROEK, EDS.

Young Adult Literature and the New Literary Theories
ANNA O. SOTER

Literacy Matters
ROBERT P. YAGELSKI

Children's Inquiry
JUDITH WELLS LINDFORS

Close to Home
JUAN C. GUERRA

Life at the Margins
JULIET MERRIFIELD ET AL.

Literacy for Life
HANNA ARLENE FINGERET & CASSANDRA DRENNON

The Book Club Connection
SUSAN I. MCMAHON & TAFFY E. RAPHAEL, EDS., ET AL.

Until We Are Strong Together
CAROLINE E. HELLER

Writing Superheroes
ANNE HAAS DYSON

Opening Dialogue
MARTIN NYSTRAND ET AL.

Just Girls
MARGARET J. FINDERS

The First R
MICHAEL F. GRAVES, PAUL VAN DEN BROEK, &
BARBARA M. TAYLOR, EDS.

Talking Their Way into Science
KAREN GALLAS

The Languages of Learning
KAREN GALLAS

Partners in Learning
CAROL LYONS, GAY SU PINNELL, & DIANE DEFORD

Social Worlds of Children Learning to Write
in an Urban Primary School
ANNE HAAS DYSON

Inside/Outside
MARILYN COCHRAN-SMITH & SUSAN L. LYTLE

Whole Language Plus
COURTNEY B. CAZDEN

Learning to Read
G. BRIAN THOMPSON & TOM NICHOLSON, EDS.

Engaged Reading
JOHN T. GUTHRIE & DONNA E. ALVERMANN

Reading Time

The Literate Lives of Urban Secondary Students and Their Families

Catherine Compton-Lilly

Foreword by Kevin Leander

Teachers College, Columbia University
New York and London

This research was funded by Teacher Research Grants from the International Reading Association and the National Council of Teachers of English.

Published by Teachers College Press, 1234 Amsterdam Avenue, New York, NY 10027

Library of Congress Cataloging-in-Publication Data

Compton-Lilly, Catherine.
Reading time: the literate lives of urban secondary students and their families / By Catherine Compton-Lilly.
   pages cm.—(Language and literacy series)
Includes bibliographical references and index.
ISBN 978-0-8077-5303-3 (pbk. : alk. paper)
ISBN 978-0-8077-5304-0 (hardcover : alk. paper)
      1. Urban youth—Education–United States—Case studies. 2. Urban youth—Books and reading—United States—Case studies. 3. Middle school students—Books and reading—United States—Case studies. 4. Reading—Parent participation—United States–Case studies. 5. Education, Urban—United States—Case studies. I. Title.
LC5131.C616 2012
370.9173'20973—dc23

ISBN 978-0-8077-5303-3 (paperback)
ISBN 978-0-8077-5304-0 (hardcover)

Printed on acid-free paper
Manufactured in the United States of America

19 18 17 16 15 14 13 12   8 7 6 5 4 3 2 1

Contents

Foreword

As I reflect on *Reading Time* I am taken in my feelings and thoughts to two places. The first is back to the Western Wall in Jerusalem, which I had the great pleasure to visit the holy city two years ago. Like countless others—some with religious fervor, some as pilgrims, some as mere curious tourists—I hand wrote short prayers for the futures of my kids on small slips of paper, rolled them up, and slipped them into the cracks between the stones. Many of the stones extend in time nearly four millennia, to the era of King Solomon. Placing my hands on the stones in prayer helped me feel that a timeless God was reading my notes and looking after the future of my children.

The second place I am taken, in my imagination, also involves the writing out of notes and letters. Yet, in this case thousands of people en masse are placing their notes into a large urn at the culmination of the All Souls Procession in Tucson, Arizona. These notes, written by people of different cultures, beliefs, and histories, are prayers or reflections for those who have passed on before. Also written up are different phases of life, experiences, practices, and relationships of the past that are being recognized, memorialized, and ritualized, to be consumed in the flames of the urn. Both of these places and sets of practices capture something at least of the spirit of *Reading Time*, where it is claimed that a reading of time is essentially important for an understanding of reading itself. Indeed, these practices illustrate well a dominant theme by Catherine Compton-Lilly throughout this provocative book: texts and literacy practices are somehow stuck in the stones or caught up in the flames of multiple temporalities. Conversely, our experiences of time are set not only by clocks and calendars, but also by letters, books, and web pages. The temporal chicken and the reading egg vie for position.

This tight knit relationship of literacy and time presents us all kinds of exciting problems and possibilities for literacy research, which Compton-Lilly examines through longitudinal case studies and theory-building. Two current complex issues in literacy scholarship strike me as particularly "timely" and as re-invigorated. Compton-Lilly examines how the identity and learning relationship is not at all evident when identity and learning are methodologically locked into the same constrained contextual container of a research study. Rather, certain identity practices and artifacts (for example, identification with specific books and reading preferences) appear to carry across generations, perhaps affording opportunities to learn for case study participants but not being linked to timescales of learning. Temporalities associated with identity seem well out of step with those of schooling in the study, prompting us to re-examine the tensions of learning and identification, and in particular those that affect the lives of those under-served by school, such as the urban poor in Compton-Lilly's research. Moreover, identity trajectories related to literacy, documented in case study children over 10-year time spans, are not uni-directional. The category of becoming a reader, for instance, ebbs and flows and changes over the life course along with desires and other social practices, and is not a mere passage through which one moves.

With respect to her rich data selections that span 10 years in the lives of children, which contrast children's histories to those of their parents, Compton-Lilly's work convincingly extends previous calls for longitudinal studies in interpretive literacy research. The book features compelling examples of literacy practices that traverse generations (e.g., specific discourses concerning schooling and texts), which could only be understood through interviews and observations extending over time. Beyond a general claim calling for longitudinal study, Compton-Lilly lays out specific directions that are especially compelling for the development of theory and methodology in literacy research. Among them, she introduces and puts to use a multi-temporal methodology for literacy research, a methodology that "reads time" in social practices, in discourses, in the movements of artifacts, in texts, in institutional structures, and in interactions. The senses and experiences of time in these diverse sites begin to be articulated such that questions of "what is time made of" and "how do we see time" are opened up and reimagined. Moreover, Compton-Lilly compellingly underscores how such questions are not merely theoretical quandaries. Rather, these are critical social quandaries, in that Dominant Discourses with long histories, including discourses of race, have powerful holds on the movements of children through time.

—Kevin Leander, Vanderbilt University

Acknowledgments

I would again like to first thank the students and families who welcome me back during each phase of this study. I am extremely grateful for their generosity and their willingness to allow me to share their words with others. I am constantly in awe of their strength and commitment.

A teacher research grant from the International Reading Association funded this phase of the research project, and I am grateful to this organization for their continuing support of my work. I would also like to thank the editorial staff at Teachers College Press, particularly Meg Lemke and Susan Liddicoat, for their help and unending faith. Finally, I am very grateful for an amazing group of colleagues at the University of Wisconsin–Madison. Among them, I must thank Maggie Hawkins, Beth Graue, Mariana Pacheco, Erica Halverson, Michael Thomas, Constance Steinkuehler, Dawnene Hassett, and Mary Louise Gomez.

Finally, I continuously thank my family, Dr. Todd Lilly and Miss Carly Lilly, for helping me to follow my dreams and joining me on the journey.

Introducing Time

Over 10 years ago when I began a study of my 1st-grade students and their families, I wanted to understand and document their understanding about reading, its purposes in their lives, and the ways they viewed themselves as readers. However, as I have returned again and again to visit and interview my former students and their families, various dimensions of temporality have become evident and compelling. Students and parents revisited experiences from their past, compared the past to the present, spoke of the pace of instruction, described progress in school, and their hopes for the future. Each of these conversations referenced time—the past, the present, pace, progress, and the future. Based on these accounts, I argue that humans are temporal beings, and that time plays a significant role in literacy learning, identity construction, and schooling. While I have not abandoned my interest in reading, I have come to view reading practices as evolving and changing over time within complex contexts that involve interactions with the past, as they are enacted in the present, with an eye to the future.

While time is a constant and inescapable dimension of life, little research has been done to examine how people take on ways of being, valuing, and knowing across long periods of time. How does time function as a contextual factor in our lives? How do we make sense of our experiences based on the past and as we live in the present? What do we take from the past, how do we envision the future? And how does time matter? How do we make sense of our lives over time?

Educational practitioners and researchers have generally failed to recognize and examine the ways people draw upon time as they move through their lives. In most U.S. schools, students are grouped by grade level and placed with a particular teacher for a semester or a year. Educators focus on having students meet grade-level competencies, pass grade-level tests, and be promoted to the next grade. Meeting these benchmarks is tied to time. Being promoted to 3rd grade is not just about what a student knows, it is about what the student must know at a particular point in time. Students' and teachers' lives are segmented into school years, semesters, class periods, and literacy blocks. When time is segmented and only short periods of time are monitored, educators, policy makers, and researchers often fail to consider students' long-term trajectories. Schools are not well-structured to attend to students' longitudinal experiences.

Educational researchers are also generally guilty of neglecting time. Beginning with our dissertation studies, educational researchers tend to focus on 1- or 2-year studies. Expectations related to completing a dissertation, finding a faculty position, and then obtaining tenure make longitudinal projects appear impractical and perhaps impossible. In addition, funding opportunities for longitudinal qualitative research that extend beyond 3 years are rare. Together with schooling practices that neatly sort students' school experiences into grade levels, semesters, and marking periods, professional expectations related to educational research and publication discourage educational researchers from conducting research that attends to students' experiences over long periods of time.

In this book, I argue that time matters in education. It is only by attending to the experiences of students and their families over time that we can make sense of students' school trajectories and begin to envision school experiences that support students not just at particular points in time but across meaningful and worthwhile educational careers.

TIME AND LITERACY RESEARCH

While time has been referenced in educational research, it has not been treated as a central construct in literacy research. In the following section, I review some of the ways literacy researchers have recognized time.

Some literacy researchers have conducted longitudinal studies that involve participants within particular communities over long periods of time. For example, Heath (1983) conducted what is perhaps the quintessential example of long-term qualitative research. Between 1969 and 1978, Heath lived with and worked alongside children and families in two Carolina communities. She examined oral language traditions and literacy practices through careful, long-term observation and thoughtful interaction with participants. More recently, Heath (2001) returned to this community to document changes that have occurred since her initial study. In a second classic longitudinal study, beginning in 1977 and extending through the early 1980s, Taylor (1983) documented literacy practices in six families as children learned to read and write. While Taylor recognized the existence of "conservation and change in the transmission of literacy styles and values" (p. 7), and documented the role parents' memories played in their present literacy practices, time was peripheral to her analysis of emergent and variable literacy practices. She did not recognize or examine how children and their parents live, act, interact, read, and write within time.

Reese, Kroesen, and Gallimore (2000) collected qualitative and quantitative data to examine the agential behavior of immigrant Latino families in Los Angeles. Over the course of this 10-year longitudinal study, they focused on the identification of behaviors that led to school success. More recently, long-term longitudinal research has been conducted in international contexts including Australian high schools (McLeod & Yates, 2006) and elementary schools (Comber, Badger, Barnett, Nixon, & Pitt, 2002). McLeod and Yates (2006) followed students over 8 years as they moved through secondary school. Specifically, they examined the development of dispositions, attitudes, and identities as well as the effects of schooling on students. Comber and her colleagues (2002) examined the literacy development of children from low socioeconomic backgrounds between the ages 5 and 10. They documented the literacy practices of children and analyzed assessment data. While these studies share longitudinal methods to explore issues such as agency, identity, attitudes, and literacy development, they have not explicitly attended to time as a contextual dimension of children's experiences. In other words, they have not explored how children live within and make sense of experiences across time.

Other researchers have attended to the sociohistorical nature of time within short-term projects. Gutiérrez (2007) highlighted the cultural-historical nature of learning and development; "literacy learning is not an individual accomplishment, and instead is built on a long history of relationships and influences, both local and distal" (p. 116). Lanehart (2002) documented the stories from three generations of women in her family to explore themes related to language, literacy, identity, and education. Enciso (2007) examined history as an interpretive frame in literacy education and sociocultural research. She argued that there is an illusion of a unified and accessible past that teachers draw upon to create the interpretive frames they use to make sense of the world. She maintained that teachers and researchers must apply more critical analyses of memory and imagination to their work. Finally, Pahl (2007) applied the construct of timescales to literacy learning in immigrant families. She examined a child's artistic depiction of a bird as a semiotic artifact that crossed multiple timescales—from the immediacy of his current home and school experiences to his family's history and a larger cultural history of migration, flight, and relocation. These studies have contributed to the beginnings of a line of research that conceptualizes time as context.

In this book, I explicitly attend to time as a context that situates literacy and identity construction for my former students. Unlike previous analyses of children and schooling, I place time at the center of discussions about reading practices, identities, reading achievement, and literacy to document some of the ways people access resources across time to make sense of themselves, literacy practices, and their worlds. By focusing on children over a long period of time, I was able to observe processes and patterns that would have remained invisible in shorter projects, and use these insights to reflect on how time operates in students' lives and families' experiences.

HOW DOES TIME IMPACT STUDENTS AND FAMILIES?

Based on my work with families over the past decade, I offer five premises that when combined, begin to explain the significance of time for educational and literacy researchers and educators.

1. People's understandings of the world are constructed, refined, revised, and abandoned over time. Learning is a process of adding to and/or revising what people have known and understood in the past. Current learning builds on past experiences by extending existing ideas, challenging past understandings, refining insights, and abandoning theories and insights that no longer work. What people know and believe has relevance to possible futures that they envision for themselves and others.

2. Understandings of self are constructed over time, and individuals draw upon past experiences, as well as future goals, as they situate themselves in relation to family, peer, and school expectations. Identities, roles, and positionings are all assumed and reworked over time as individuals encounter other people and institutions, as well as available resources and options. Identities involve enactments (i.e., behaviors, discourses, alliances, literacy practices) that can be adopted or rejected as various identities and roles are assumed and dismissed.

3. Institutional time, related to teaching and learning, determines the duration of learning experiences, the pacing of instruction, and official expectations relative to time (i.e., criteria for promotion, competencies, test scores, report cards, marking periods).

4. People are "temporal beings" who are caught up within multiple dimensions of time—shared social histories, their personal pasts, and ongoing experiences. However, schools and research communities generally fail to acknowledge and attend to the ways people experience time and make sense of their experiences across time.

5. Because schools and educational research projects are generally organized to deal with groups of students for relatively short periods of time, information and understanding

are lost in not being able to observe, document, and analyze long-term learning, reading practices, identity construction, and the cumulative effect of institutional practices and policies on students and their families.

Together, these five premises recognize time as a contextual dimension that affects people's understandings of both the world and of themselves. The temporal expectations of schools and research institutions have limited the opportunity, and perhaps the ability, to attend to time as a contextual factor in the lives of students despite the fact that time is a fundamental aspect of everyone's experiences as human beings.

THE STUDENTS AND FAMILIES IN THIS STUDY

This book takes us on a rich journey. The insights described in this volume build upon previous work with the same group of students, as noted above. The first phase occurred when eight of the nine students described in this book were students in my 1st-grade classroom. This phase, which was designed as a 1-year teacher research project, explored the concepts about reading held by my inner-city 1st-grade students and their parents (Compton-Lilly, 2003). Four years later, I became curious about the progress of my former students, and returned to visit the same families when the children were in grades 4 and 5; this second phase focused more broadly on literacy and schooling paying more attention to identity, schooling, and school success (Compton-Lilly, 2007b). In the current book, I have again returned to visit my former students and their families. At the time of these interviews, the students were in grades 7 and 8.

In all, 11 families participated in my longitudinal research study. Although only nine of these families remained in the study during the middle school year, all of the students appear in this book and thus are introduced below; see Appendix A for additional information about the families.

At the start of the project, David lived with his mother, Ms. Johnson, his younger brother, and older siblings. David is biracial; his mother is European American, and his father, who passed away the summer after David was in my class, was African American. Ms. Johnson grew up in a middle-class home in a small town outside the city where she and her family currently reside. Tall and thin, with a charming smile, David was popular with his teachers and did well in school. David often spoke enthusiastically about school and the books he was assigned to read. He spoke of someday starting his own business, and was constantly describing his plans to get rich.

When Christy was in my 1st-grade class, she lived with her mother, Ms. Green, and Christy's younger sister. Christy's mother is White, and her father is African American. Christy's mother was diagnosed during adolescence with bipolar disorder. Christy's father saw Christy and her sister a couple times each year. Christy had been retained in 1st grade the year before she was in my class. By the time Christy was in 5th grade, Ms. Green had remarried. Ms. Green's new husband had a criminal record, and Christy and her sister were removed from the home by social workers. They were placed in foster care where they remained for 3 years until they were legally adopted. Christy's new family included her adopted mother, Ms. Denver, several foster and adopted siblings, as well as a biological daughter and grown children who lived down the street from her new family. Christy is a quiet, cautious girl who often spoke of her biological mom during the interviews.

Jermaine had a grown older sister and an older brother. He lived with his mother and father, Mr. and Mrs. Hudson. Jermaine is African American. His mother grew up in an urban area about an hour's drive from the research city. His father grew up in the rural South. Jermaine's father was older than Jermaine's mother and had dropped out of school to work. He later became a nurse and performed as a drummer with a jazz band. Jermaine struggled in school—failing grades 1 and 7. Nonetheless, he continued to identify schoolbooks that he enjoyed.

During the early interviews, Peter lived with his mother, Ms. Horner, and younger brother. Peter is African American. When Peter was in 5th grade, his mother remarried, and Peter's sister was born. During 8th grade, the family moved to New York City, but returned within a few months when his mother and stepfather divorced. Peter moved in with his biological father and later lived with his grandmother. Peter was an excellent student who loved reading science fiction.

When Bradford was in 1st grade, he lived with his mother, Ms. Holt, five older brothers, and an older sister. At that time, all of the children were living at home. By middle school, only Bradford and his older brother were still living at home. Bradford is African American and the first child in his family to have difficulties with the law. He spent several weeks in a youth detention facility for being caught holding a bag of marijuana when a group of older boys abandoned him just as the police arrived. Bradford did not like to read and struggled with reading throughout his school career.

Alicia is African American, although her mother had a Spanish surname (Rodriguez) from an earlier marriage. Alicia lived with her mother, four older brothers, and younger sister. Since her early elementary years, she had been a step team member—first at a community center and later at her school. While Alicia complained about the books she read in middle school, she had been an avid reader in 1st grade and read teenage romances novels at home.

When Javon was in middle school, he lived with his mother, Ms. Mason, twin brother, and a younger brother. During earlier phases of the research project, older siblings and sometimes cousins had also lived in the home. Javon, an African American student, generally did well in school. As his mother explained, his school achievement improved, and he was getting along with his teachers. He read mysteries and horror books at home, but complained about some of the books they were assigned to read in school.

Although Marvin had an older sister who lived with the family when he was in 1st grade, she moved out when she was 16. In middle school, it was just Marvin and his grandparents, Mr. and Ms. Sherwood. Marvin and his sister were adopted by their grandparents when Marvin was 5 years old. Marvin was a quiet awkward child who sometimes got into trouble at school. Like his grandfather, he read the newspaper almost every day. Marvin found reading difficult but was supported by his grandmother, who helped him at home. Marvin is African American.

Tiffany was involved in the research project only during 1st grade. She lived with her mother, Ms. Webster, and brother. At the beginning of 1st grade, Tiffany struggled with reading but ended the year reading on grade level. The family moved and could not be located. Tiffany is biracial (Middle Eastern and European American).

Jasmine, a Puerto Rican student, lived with her mother, Ms. Hernandez, younger brother, and father. By the time I returned to conduct the 5th-grade interviews, her father was no longer living in the home. Jasmine was a strong reader in 1st grade, but according to her mother, she started to fall behind in grade 4. Jasmine and her family could not be located for the middle school interviews.

Angela was added to the sample in grade 5, when her younger sister was a student in my 1st-grade class. Angela is European American. Like her parents, Mr. and Mrs. Burns, she was an avid reader. She did well in school and was planning to either attend college or become a tattoo artist. Her sister, Meg, and her mother voraciously read series books. Angela was the only student in the sample whose family moved to a suburban area outside of the city.

When I studied these children when they were in elementary school, I did not realize that the experiences of my students related to schooling, identity, literate identity, and school success all involved time. It was when the children were in middle school, and I had spent the better part of a decade working with them, that I started to recognize temporal aspects of their experiences.

ORGANIZATION OF THIS BOOK

In this book, I focus on time as a contextual dimension of literacy, learning, and schooling. As Saldaña (2003) explains, documenting change over time is a unique contribution that longitudinal qualitative research makes to the field of education. In Chapter 1, I introduce Javon to illustrate the five temporal premises, presented above. I then present a theoretical framework that situates discourses, cultural models, and artifacts as operating across multiple timescales (Lemke, 2000, 2001, 2005). I apply this theoretical framework to reveal temporal aspects of educational contexts.

In Chapter 2, I explore the changes that have occurred for the families that have been involved in this 8-year project. I focus on their moving to new homes and neighborhoods, changes within families, and students moving into middle school.

Chapter 3 describes the reading practices of students over the course of the 8-year project. I examine various influences on students' reading preferences including series books, media and technology, magazines, and the convergences that often exist between students' and parents' reading preferences.

In Chapter 4, I offer insights into relationships between teachers and students across time. I begin by presenting accounts of students' favorite teachers. I then explore how students describe time as operating in classrooms in terms of teachers providing time, making time, taking time, and giving time. I end with concerns voiced by students in relation to teacher authority and boring classes.

Chapter 5 documents the ways parents draw on memories of the past as they make sense of their children's school experiences. Memories of "Dick and Jane" open this chapter as some parents nostalgically recall those memorable books. I then explore *now and then* discourses and the ways race is featured in some of these accounts. Parents tell stories of favorite teachers that reflect the ways they and their children make sense of children's ongoing school experiences. The chapter ends with concerns parents voice as they age relative to their children's young teachers.

Chapter 6 explores the vocational aspirations of students when they were in grade 1 and in middle school. I then explore the ways parents position their children as *good kids* despite the challenges some children faced. I describe the trust that many families appear to have in their children's schools. The chapter ends with the dreams that some students hold for possible futures.

In Chapter 7, the case study of Alicia is used to examine literate identity construction as Alicia moves through school. The ways Alicia constructs herself as a reader and as a person are both recursive and future-oriented.

As this case study illustrates, Alicia's literacy practices are situated within complex dimensions of race, schooling, and literacy learning. The chapter examines life experiences, family stories, literacy practices, and larger historical accounts that contribute to Alicia's identity construction as a student and as a reader.

In the book's Conclusion, I return to the five temporal premises that were presented earlier, explore how the accounts presented in this book relate to those premises, and provide significant insights into the longitudinal experiences of students. I then present suggestions for teachers, administrators, and policy makers who are interested in attending to the temporal experiences of students. The ultimate goal of this chapter is to present readers with possibilities for thinking about students' current educational trajectories and designing more beneficial experiences for the future.

CHAPTER 1

Time, Theory, and Javon

During the 8 years of my longitudinal study of a group of children who had been my 1st-grade students, and their families, I was able to witness how time manifested itself in their lives. Parents recounted memories about school and told stories about their parents and grandparents. I was told accounts of events I remembered, or remembered hearing about during earlier interviews. I reflected on student's memories of my 1st-grade classroom, alongside their accounts of more recent school experiences. I watched as families changed; babies were born; parents, grandparents, and great grandparents "passed on"; children were adopted into new families; older siblings dropped out of school or headed off to college; and parents married. Unanticipated events occurred; some were marvelous and others were traumatic.

I learned that time is a critical contextual factor in the lives of students, and attending to students' experiences of time and the understandings they construct over time can significantly inform educational research, policy, and practice. Although my longitudinal work with students and their families has provided many insights into their reading practices and attitudes, more importantly, it has revealed significant gaps in the ways educators have attended to students' literacy and school trajectories.

In this chapter, I draw on a case study of Javon to illustrate some of the temporal lessons that my research has revealed. I then present a set of theoretical tools that I bring to the longitudinal data presented in this book.

FIVE TEMPORAL PREMISES AND JAVON'S STORY

Javon's case illustrates the five temporal premises that I presented in the Introduction to this book; to review:

1. Time is intricately connected to understandings of the world and literacy learning.
2. Understandings about self are assumed over time.
3. Institutional policies regarding teaching and learning are related to time.

4. Humans are temporal beings who simultaneously draw upon multiple dimensions of time.
5. Schools and research initiatives bring their own particular temporal expectations and practices.

Time Is Intricately Connected to Understandings of the World and Literacy Learning

New learning, including literacy learning, always exists in relationship to what is known. As students move through school, and as researchers progress through their professional careers, understandings of the world are constructed, refined, and revised. Learning is a process of adding to what people have known and understood in the past as they conceptualize the present and the future, extending existing ideas, challenging past understandings, refining insights, and abandoning theories and insights that no longer make sense or hold true.

When Javon was in 1st grade, he identified the *Ugly Duckling* and the *Three Little Pigs* as his favorite books; his preference for these folktales is related to time. These stories are artifacts that have rich temporal links not only to Javon's preschool experiences, when adults read these stories to him, but also to the role these folktales may have played in the childhood literacy experiences of prior generations, including his parents. Being exposed to classic texts is an expectation for young children and marker of their development. In my 1st-grade classroom, when Javon was able to read these texts independently, it was evidence of his accomplishments as a reader. As Frank Smith argued (1987), Javon was becoming a member of the "literacy club."

At age 6, Javon voiced commonly accepted discourses about the importance of reading. He reported that reading "helps you learn" and "gets you into grades"; he maintained that if you learn to read "you get a job." Javon was already articulating dominant discourses about the importance of reading and linking literacy abilities to both school and vocational success. Reading was a marker of personal competency. To Javon, it was easy and fun because the books "got words you know." He believed he was a good reader because, "I be getting books a lot of times at home." Even in 1st grade, Javon recognized the capital embodied in reading and owning large numbers of books.

By 5th grade, Javon preferred adventure books, mysteries, and ghost tales. His favorite books were from the *Fear Street* Series by R. L. Stine (Stine, 1989–1997). Javon and his twin brother exchanged these books with each other and their friends. His book preferences had settled along gender lines and reflected the dominant reading preferences of preteen boys—specifically, horror. By all accounts, Javon was an avid reader. Ms.

Mason, Javon's mother, recreated a typical interaction that occurred when Javon found a book he enjoyed.

> "Ma, I want my book. What happened to my book? I want to read it. I want to read it." I [Ms. Mason] told him. I said, "I'm so happy to see that you can read long books now". . . . He was surprised when he finished a whole chapter of it. I told him. I said, "You're doing good, boy." I said, "Keep it up."

Commonly accepted discourses that connected reading and attainment were apparent in discourses voiced in Javon's family. Ms. Mason encouraged all her children to read and identified herself as an avid reader. She reported that she purchased a lot of books, "because I'm the type of person, I love books. So, I usually buy a lot of books." Like her children, Ms. Mason preferred mystery and horror novels.

Javon continued to consider himself a good reader, explaining, "I'll be reading on mostly hard words." This comment voiced in grade 5 echoed statements from 1st grade, highlighting the importance of learning to read in terms of education, grades, and intelligence:

> "Learning [to read] helps you in your education."
> "[It] helps you get the higher grade."
> [People who read] "become smarter" and "more intelligent."

Javon noted that he was earning As, Bs, and Cs on his report card and making his mother proud.

In 8th grade, Javon continued to earn As and Bs in school, but described himself as less interested in reading. He still enjoyed action novels, *Harry Potter* books (Rowling, 1997–2007), and *Holes* (Sachar, 1998). Javon identified J. K. Rowling as his favorite author, but admitted that he had not read the most recent book in the series. While he read books that were assigned in school and reported that he appreciated most of them, Javon did not like to read "a lot" and noted that he read only when he "had to." At school, Javon had read three books by Walter Dean Myers and *The Lord of the Rings* (Tolkien, 1954); Javon noted that these were good books contrasting them with *Lieutenant Hornblower* (Forester, 1951)—a book he did not enjoy. He reported that his friends did not like to read "because they say they got other things to do." As Javon explained, "I'll read when the teachers tell me to. But if they don't tell me, I won't read." While he had read the *Lord of the Rings*, he was not interested in seeing the movie that was recently released. Ms. Mason reported that he was spending more time with his video games and did not visit the public library.

Clearly learning to read and becoming a reader was a process for Javon. During each round of interviews, we observe Javon not only engaging with increasingly challenging texts, but also learning about the role reading plays in his world. In 1st grade, Javon enjoyed the traditional tales that he read at school and described reading as critical for both school and employment. His interest was in learning to read, and he took pride in positioning himself as a competent reader. By 5th grade, he and his brother enjoyed horror books that reflected the reading preferences of their friends and their mother. While Javon and his brother shared his mother's interest in mysteries and horror, they did not simply adopt her reading preferences. Javon was simultaneously reading books that were popular with his peers (e.g., *Holes* by Sachar, 1998). By 8th grade, Javon choose not to read, and like his friends, he had "other things to do." He voiced animosity toward school-assigned books. However, despite his insistence that he only read assigned books, he admitted that he enjoyed many of the books.

Javon's understanding about reading changed over time. These understandings involved much more than self-assessment of his reading ability. They were constructed within complex interactions involving school, home, friends, and family members. Reading also involved dominant and rarely questioned discourses that described literacy as both a means to education and employment. Javon's enthusiasm for traditional folktales evolved into an interest in *Harry Potter* and action novels. Meeting school criteria for reading increasingly involved books that did not interest Javon. Over time, these understandings about reading also involved contradictory positionings relative to practices and preferences—being an avid reader at one point in time and a self-described reluctant reader a few years later.

Understandings About Self Are Assumed Over Time

The lessons that Javon was learning about reading involved identity construction. His reading choices were enactments of self. The identities he assumed and the actions he took, including the books he chose and rejected, reflected choices he made as he encountered people and acted within institutions. Cultural expectations about being a reader, being male, and being a student are all reflected in his actions.

Javon's reading of the *Fear Street* books (Stine, 1989–1997) with their simple plots developed into reading books with long lists of characters and complicated plots that extended across multiple volumes (i.e., *Lord of the Rings, Harry Potter*). Javon's literacy learning was not limited to growth in his reading ability or skill with comprehending complex texts; Javon was also learning about being a reader and how that positioning intersected with his identity as a student and his peer affiliations. Javon challenged his past ways of being a reader, and abandoned practices that no longer worked for him as he assumed new identities relative to peers, reading, and school. He rejected folktales in favor of mystery and horror—genres that resonated not only with being male but also reflected the popular media. Javon enacted cultural models related to reading and the types of people who read particular types of books.

Ms. Mason recognized the potential influence of peers and drew on her own past to understand Javon's experiences (Rogers, 2003; Taylor, 1983). She worried that other kids might not only get her son into trouble, but also might "discourage him or something" from doing well in school. She referenced her own experiences when she spoke with her children about school, "I put myself in my kid." While it had been over 30 years since Ms. Mason had been in middle school, she explained, "Yes, when I was younger, sometimes when you have a group of friends or whatever, then you sit and blunder around thinking that [what they want to do] is wrong. And [you] try [to] be, I want to be with that group so I'm going to go ahead and do it. Try and get away with it." Self and personal experiences were embedded in the ways Ms. Mason made sense of Javon's experiences in school and with his peers. Time was critical as Ms. Mason drew on her own experiences and shared these experiences with Javon to provide him with tools that he could use to make sense of himself and the world.

Occasionally during the interviews, students called upon me to contribute to their understandings of themselves over time. When Javon was in my 1st-grade class, he was often in trouble. Javon was popular with the other students and would regularly distract them when they were supposed to be working or paying attention in class. At that time, Ms. Mason worked at the childcare center that was attached to our school. On particularly difficult mornings, Javon and Ms. Mason both remember me escorting Javon to his mother's office to discuss his behavior. When I spoke with his mother years later, she assured me that Javon was no longer getting in trouble in school, "I think because he got older and he calmed down a lot, and I think that he cares more about his personality and then he acts more mature."

When Javon was in 8th grade, he also recalled the difficulties he had in 1st grade and asked me why I had chosen him for the project. To my surprise, his mother explained that Javon had told her that he worried that he had been "busy" in my 1st-grade class when I had selected students for the project and mistakenly suspected that his participation was some sort of punishment for bad classroom behavior. In this incident, Javon's understandings of himself as a research participant was constructed as he drew upon his experiences in 1st grade to make sense of his experiences in the present—in this case, ongoing visits from his former 1st-grade teacher.

Throughout the interviews, Javon enacted his evolving identity through reported reading practices at school, with family members and with peers. Javon was engaged in identity work that revealed how the identities, roles, and positionings that he assumed were reworked and revisited. As noted previously, Javon went from describing himself as an engaged reader in 1st grade to identifying boundaries and affiliations with peers that did not involve reading in middle school. The schoolbooks that he enjoyed in 1st grade became assigned books, and the little boy who regularly got into trouble in 1st grade became a calmer, more mature middle school student who was suspicious of my motivations in choosing him for the research project. Javon referenced the past as he worked to make sense of himself across time and in the present. Identities involve enactments (i.e., behaviors, discourses, alliances, literacy practices), and Javon, like all of us, constantly enacted various practices and positionings as he revisited, adapted, adopted, and dismissed past ways of being.

Institutional Policies Regarding Teaching and Learning Are Related to Time

Following students for long periods of time as they moved through school drew my attention to the ways time is allocated in educational institutions. Time affects learning and schooling in a myriad of ways including the duration of lessons, the pacing of instruction, grade level expectations, retention and promotion, educational standards, and passing tests. As did all of my former students, Javon experienced the temporal expectations of schooling.

The school district in which Javon attended middle school had adopted a literacy reform project that encouraged teachers to set reading goals for students based on the number of books students read. Students in each class competed to meet their reading goals. Javon found this process frustrating; he told me, "We [each student] got to read 25 books before the end of the school year." At the time of the fall interview he had read only five books. He complained that the teachers "like to rush us." While 25 books may seem like an admirable goal, it discouraged Javon from reading the *Harry Potter* books that he enjoyed. While he had read the first few *Harry Potter* books and owned the next book in the series, he had not started to read it. He worried that reading a book the length of *Harry Potter* would prevent him from reaching his 25-book goal; temporal expectations related to reading large numbers of books over relatively short periods of time contributed to Javon's not reading longer more complex books—including *Harry Potter*.

Javon's biggest frustration in middle school was the *hall sweep*. As he explained at passing time between classes "you got two minutes to get to class and if you don't, you gotta come back to school on Friday." As soon as the bell rang to begin each class, teachers and administrators would patrol the halls liberally assigning Friday detentions to students who were not in class. Javon explained that he was caught in a hall sweep last year because to get to his locker "you gotta run up and down the stairs." While the need for policies that encourage students to get to class on time and to read many books are self-evident, strict temporal expectations are rampant in schools.

Class periods, passing time, organizing courses to cover massive amounts of material, and the idea that the number of books read is the criteria for reading excellence contribute to the temporal frenzy that often exists in school. Little attention has been paid to students' reading preferences, social affiliations, interests, or identities. In addition, as will be explored in the following section, cultural differences exist in the ways people allocate and attend to time. While schools often adhere to efficiency models (Callahan, 1962) that value coordination and efficient use of time, other models exist that privilege personal relationships over temporal expectations.

Humans Are Temporal Beings Who Simultaneously Draw Upon Multiple Dimensions of Time

A premise of the book is that we are all *temporal beings* who draw on multiple dimensions of time. At times we may call on events and experiences from our own past or we may reflect on the history lessons we learn in school; at other times we draw on stories that we have been told about our parents or grandparents, brothers, or sisters. Despite the continual references we make to events across timescales, schools and research communities generally fail to acknowledge and attend to the ways people are situated in time.

However, there is always the possibility that just as Ms. Mason drew on her own experiences in school, teachers can draw upon their pasts to highlight their own humanity. Javon described a favorite teacher, Mr. Whitney, "Like he don't try to act [fake], he tells [us] what's going on and he tells like the truth and stuff. He tells us what types fights he's been in or stuff like that." While Javon reassures me that they do work hard in Mr. Whitney's class, he explained, that "sometimes if we really good, he lets us sit around and talk for a couple of minutes." Multiple temporal issues operate in this account. First, like the teachers described by Metcalfe and Game (2007), Mr. Whitney presented himself as a temporal being who brought a real and relevant past to his teaching. He does not present himself as a teacher, but as a person who has made various decisions at different points in his life. His humanity is evidenced by his willingness to acknowledge and publicly share his past. Second, Mr. Whitney was willing to devote time at the end of class to talk with his students. He recognized that schooling and learning entailed more than teaching information and time on task. It involves taking time to know students as individuals who have experiences beyond the present moment of the classroom (Genishi & Dyson, 2009). Mr. Whitney's actions also reference possible literate futures for his students—my past was like yours, thus your future could resemble mine.

Mr. Whitney positioned himself within time when he shared his past with his students. Rather than negating or ignoring his past, he presented himself as a person contextualized in time, and used this positioning to foster relationships with students. Living in and through time is uniquely human. By drawing across multiple temporal dimensions (e.g., Mr. Whitney's past, the present, students' futures), Mr. Whitney highlighted the temporal and human nature of his experiences.

Schools and Research Projects Bring Their Own Temporal Expectations and Practices

Schools are not designed to attend to students' long-term trajectories. Grade levels with different teachers or teams of teachers and the limited numbers of opportunities that teachers have to communicate with students from prior years discourage educators from considering the long-term and cumulative effects of schooling on students. Although cumulative files are maintained, these files are generally repositories for documentation that can be used to support school decisions in relation to disciplinary measures, course placement, counseling beyond school, employment options, graduation, or expulsion. They are rarely used to explore a student's long-term school experiences to identify points of possibility and potential.

As pointed out in the Introduction, the challenges of meeting promotion requirements and obtaining funding discourage educational researchers from engaging in long-term studies. Schools and educational research agendas, and funding generally, focus on groups of students for relatively short periods of time. Much information is lost by not being able to observe, document, and analyze long-term learning, identity construction, and the cumulative effect of institutional time on students.

In considering the future, Javon explained that he will "probably" become a teacher when he gets older and suspects that he will teach social studies, "because I don't like it that much." His goal was "to make the kids learn to love it." Javon's decision to teach social studies was not grounded in his love of the subject, but as a reaction to his own school experiences. The people students become, the dreams they hold, and the challenges they face are not the results of the simple cumulation of experiences. They involve revisiting negative and positive experiences, rethinking the identities, and reworking possibilities for the future. The ways schools and research communities operate—their procedures, policies, and the structures they create—obfuscate the ways meanings are constructed over time. By focusing on groups of students for relatively short periods of time, significant information is lost and longitudinal processes related to long-term learning, identity construction, and the cumulative effect of institutional expectations of schooling are neither documented nor examined.

TIMES IN OUR LIVES: DISCOURSES, CULTURAL MODELS, ARTIFACTS, AND TIMESCALES

In this section, I consider a set of theoretical constructs that can help educators and researchers to think about how time is connected to learning and identities, as well as its relationships to people's lives, research initiatives, and educational policies. Philosophers who have written about time (Bakhtin, 1994; Heidegger, 1962; Laccour, 1980) are generally far removed from schools and classrooms. I have spent many hours seeking frameworks that are relevant to education and speak to the temporal dimensions of schooling. They do exist—Bourdieu's theory of habitus (Bourdieu & Passeron, 1977), Lemke's theory of timescales (2000, 2001, 2005), and Bakhtin's construct of chronotope (1994) all have relevance to the issues I raise. My longitudinal investigation has inspired me to look beyond traditional bodies of work that are utilized in education and to examine existing resources in new ways and from new angles.

Adam (1990), a sociologist, identified a mismatch between "social theory and social life." She noted that "when theorists focus on structure they present a world without change. When they focus on change, this is charted within a static framework which defines the boundaries of before and after" (p. 3). In other words, institutions, social contexts, communities, cultures, and individual identities are often treated as static. When changes are noted, they are often referenced in relation to particular events—before 9/11 or after the Civil War. In contrast, Adam argues for recognizing the complexity of time and seeking "relations between time, temporality, tempo and timing, between clock time, chronology, social time and time-consciousness, between motion, process, chance, continuity and the temporal modalities of past, present and future, between time as a resource, as ordering principle and as becoming of the possible, or between any combination of these" (p. 13).

In their book on researching social change, McLeod and Thomson (2009) explore these complexities in terms of research methods—examining the temporal complexities the particular research methods reveal and obfuscate. They challenge three temporal myths originally identified by Gergen (1984). Like Adam (1990), they challenge conceptualizations of social variables as static (e.g., social class as a static set of categories through which people might move). They worry that a preponderance of short-term studies limit attention to long-term patterns relative to trajectories. Longitudinal qualitative studies that involve extended time horizons have the potential to reveal insights that are not visible in shorter studies. Finally, McLeod and Thomson (2009) highlight the importance of attending to local situated meanings rather than seeking general patterns and shared understandings among participants. Attending to time means that every person brings a unique set of past experiences, current understandings, and future expectations that result in unique subjectivities and understandings of the world. The longitudinal research described in this book allows us to explore the complexity of time in the experiences of nine students, and to examine the unique ways each student is situated within time, schooling, and literacy learning.

Discourses

Discourses, because they are fashioned, adapted, rejected, and refined over time, are temporal constructs. Gee (1990) uses *Discourse* in the upper case to describe ways of being that are generally accepted within a given community or organization:

> A Discourse is a socially accepted association among ways of using language, of thinking, feeling, believing, valuing, and of acting that can be used to identify oneself as a member of a socially meaningful group or social network or to signal (that one is playing) a socially meaningful role. (p. 143)

Gee explains that people utilize various discourses as they encounter people and situations. When we meet a person, we construct a sense of the "sort" of individual we believe that person to be based on the ways they dress, and talk, as well as the roles they play. In my previous work (Compton-Lilly, 2007a), I described *Dominant Discourses* that act on and through people as they go about their daily lives. Dominant Discourses support existing and historical power structures, the institutions that sustain those power structures, promoting "pervasive social theories" (Gee, 1990, p. 139) about the distribution of material goods and beliefs. Pervasive social theories suggest that the way things are is both natural and inevitable. However, discourses have histories that relate to prior renderings of discourses and the people who enacted them.

Dominant Discourses operated in the lives of my students. Dominant Discourses about the residents of low-income, communities of color were voiced by educators, community members, and presented in official policy documents. These discourses often failed to recognize the strengths that have been documented in low-income families (Compton-Lilly, 2003, 2007a; Gadsden, 2000, 2005; Gonzalez, Moll, & Amanti, 2005; Lanehart, 2002; Moll, Amanti, Neff, & Gonzalez, 1992). It was often assumed that parents were negligent and did not care whether their children learned to read or not. Assumptions about particular groups of people, including the low-income African American, Latino, and biracial families, are grounded in historical beliefs that continue to be expressed in the media and reflected in the ways many people make sense of their worlds.

While Dominant Discourses are powerful and often entail generally accepted ways of viewing the world, they are not uncontested. *Alternative Discourses* talk back to Dominant Discourses. These discourses offer alternative explanations for people's situations and the challenges they encounter. Alternative Discourses are grounded in lived experiences and often involve rethinking unquestioned assumptions. While Dominant Discourses have long histories, Alternative Discourses of critique, revision, and re-interpretation bring their own histories—histories that have often been marginalized or silenced. Alternative Discourses about literacy question whether learning to read will lead to social and economic gains. They recognize reading as entailing more than sounding out words, and challenge the notion that there is particular cannon of books that all students should read. These Alternative Discourses are generally not as prevalent or as powerful as Dominant Discourses.

Gee (1999) maintains that "words have *histories*" (p. 54; emphasis in original). Echoing Bakhtin, he notes that words "have been in other people's mouths and on other people's pens. They have circulated through other discourses and within other institutions. They have been part of specific historical events and episodes" (p. 54). Dominant and Alternative Discourses are both products constructed across time, and both carry vestiges of prior meanings, voices, and contexts.

Cultural Models

Cultural models are another means by which historically constructed ways of being and understanding inhabit contemporary classrooms (Lemke, 1995). Gee (1999) defines cultural models as "taken for granted" theories (p. 59) about the world and describes them as, "images or storylines or descriptions of simplified worlds in which prototypical events unfold" (Gee, 1999, p. 59).

Cultural models related to literacy are complex, multifaceted, and sometimes internally contradictory (Gee, 1999). They generally reflect and support assumed understandings about the critical importance of learning to read, the usefulness of sounding out words, the sequential nature of reading instruction, and a mystique the surrounds being a good reader. Cultural models of reading entail assumptions that are generally accepted as true. While some of these cultural models may hold true for some people in some situations, these assumptions are not true for the vast majority of readers. Many people live fulfilling lives without strong literacy skills (Graff, 1979; Compton-Lilly, 2007a). Sounding out words is not the key to learning to read (Compton-Lilly, 2005). Quality reading instruction does not follow a universal sequence (Allington, 2000; Clay, 2001, 2005), and there are no mystical "good" readers who read all texts equally well.

Cultural models also capture the ways people believe things should be enacted in time. Being able to pass a particular reading test at a particular point in time, reading books at a designated reading level, and adhering to the temporal expectations of schooling (i.e., timely promotion to the next grade level, passing courses, graduating from high school) are all indicators of school success that draw on cultural models of successful readers and students. Adam (1990) explained that, "Even the most cursory look at contemporary school life reveals that everything is timed. It demonstrates that the activities and interactions of all its participants are choreographed to a symphony of buzzers and bells, timetables, schedules and deadlines" (pp. 104–105).

Differences in temporal expectations and practices are enactments of cultural models related to the expected pace of activities, the amount of time activities should take, and the points of time at which things should happen. Levine (1997), a social psychologist, explores temporal differences around the world by exploring everyday markers of time. For example, Levine compared walking speeds, the time it took to purchase a stamp, and the accuracy of clocks in 31 countries. Based on his analysis, he identified Japan and the eight countries from Western Europe as the fastest-paced countries in the world. Nonindustrialized countries from Africa, Asia, and the Middle East were among the slowest. Levine also described how some people viewed being late for appointments as a sign of success—"important people keep their underlings waiting" (p. 111). In most cultures, your status can determine how long you are expected to wait for others. Levine maintained that learning to play the "waiting game" (p. 125) can be difficult in international contexts as the rules that people follow in one cultural context may not translate to another. While Levine's work reveals that different approaches to time operate in different parts of the world, a danger lies in essentializing groups of people as either fast or slow.

Cultural models of time also involve the points of time at which things are expected to happen complicating the application of universal developmental frameworks to children from diverse communities. Spencer and Markstrom-Adams (1990) challenged the application of developmental frameworks based on White middle class patterns to the development of children from African American communities. Development displayed by White children in school is treated as normal, while African American children who do not meet established norms are treated as deficit. Spencer argues for an alternative framework that recognizes and accommodates both risk and protective factors while recognizing and valuing the expectations that operate in local and cultural communities.

In reference to schooling for African American students, Lee (2007) advocates for careful attention to content selection, sequencing, participation structures, and scaffolding that can make literacy learning activities familiar to students by drawing on the competencies that African American children bring to classrooms. While on the surface these might not appear to be temporal constructs, each construct bears temporal dimensions. As Lee argues, content selection and sequencing should be based on the past experiences of children. Experiences with familiar home literacy practices should be used to develop school literacy abilities. In addition, the ways students are invited to participate in classroom activities, the scaffolding they receive, and the pace of instruction all relate to the rate at which students can and will learn material. Similarly, Gadsden (2000, 2005) explores the intergenerational literacy practices of African American mothers and daughters. She situates the rich literacy practices of African American women across generations with larger histories of literacy learning during slavery and reconstruction. As she argues, "as a historical tool and artifact, intergenerational literacy complements all literacy studies in the potential it offers to understand the sources and derivations of beliefs and practices, the ways in which they prepare children for learning, and the opportunities they lend for literacy access and reading success" (Gadsden, 2000, p. 875).

Artifacts

Lemke (2000) argued that artifacts create local coherence across time. As he explained, multiple scales of time operate within ecological systems that include socially shared artifacts—many of these artifacts are used, reused, and repurposed across time. Artifacts contribute to both the spatial and temporal architecture of schools. The spatial architecture (Lemke, 2000) of schools involves artifacts that have historically existed and continue to exist in classrooms and the ways these things are distributed in space (i.e., books, desks, paper, writing utensils, posters, chalk/white boards). Temporal architecture (Lemke, 2000) recognizes the historicity of both spaces and the practices that fill these spaces. For example, typical school spaces were envisioned at particular historical times and designed with particular purposes and practices in mind. Dimensions of classrooms and schooling (i.e., equipment, textbooks, school schedules, curricula, academic disciplines, assessment tools, terminology) have historical meanings that bring past ways of being and knowing into contemporary classrooms. When artifacts of the past coexist with artifacts and interactions in the present, complex remixes (Dyson, 2003) of new and old result.

Preexisting ways of using old artifacts often define the ways innovative artifacts are used despite a myriad of possible affordances. For example, computer technology is often used to accomplish traditionally-defined tasks (i.e., online worksheets, multiple choice assessments) despite their numerous affordances for creating new types of learning experiences. In this project, books, textbooks, report cards, reading assessments, and even stories that are told repeatedly across the years are recognized as artifacts that span timescales. For example, a novel that was part of an ongoing homework assignment reappeared years later in the form of a fondly remembered book and a meaningful artifact in a student's reading trajectory.

The histories of schooling and social policies have left their marks on contemporary urban classrooms. Specifically, issues related to school funding (Kozol, 1991), the history of urban schooling (Cremin, 1990), cost effectiveness of schooling, and historical efforts to achieve educational efficiency (Callahan, 1962) have affected not only the physical environments of urban schools but also the distribution and availability of artifacts in schools. Thus, the presence or absence of books, computers, curricular materials, desks, and posters not only contributes to the spaces students and teachers occupy but also to the ways participants make sense of schooling and literacy.

Timescales

To make sense of this longitudinal data set, I draw upon the construct of timescales, as described by Jay Lemke, to theorize and explain the ways students draw upon the past, present, and future to make sense of their literacy and schooling experiences, and define themselves as learners and literate people. The construct of timescales (Lemke, 2000, 2001, 2005) captures the multiple levels on which time operates in people's lives, and reveals the multiple temporal worlds people inhabit as well as the meanings they construct within temporal worlds. As illustrated in Figure 1.1, timescales capture the multiple ways time operates, from short movements to larger social histories that extend over thousands of years.

According to Lemke (1995), "The language others speak to us, from childhood, shapes the attitudes and beliefs that ground how we use all our powers of action" (p. 1). Individual voices are fashioned out of available social resources as people appropriate multiple discourses to serve their own

Figure 1.1: A Sampling of Timescales Relevant to Schooling

Rapidly Occurring Events	
Taking a step Speaking a word Glancing at an object	A matter of seconds
Speaking a sentence Turning around Turning a page	A minute
Verbal exchange Reciting a stanza Giving directions	A few minutes
Lesson Lunch period Bus ride	Several minutes
School day	Several hours
Slowly Occurring Events	
Lesson sequence Unit	Several days
Marking period Semester	Weeks and months
School year	Months
Elementary school years Middle school years	Years
School trajectory	More than a decade
School trajectories of family members Recent educational history	Multiple decades
School trajectories of ancestors Extended educational histories	Century
History of schooling in America	Centuries
History of schooling in Education	Millennium

purposes and make sense of their worlds. As Bakhtin (1981) maintains, "The word does not exist in a neutral and impersonal language . . . but rather it exists in other people's mouths, and in other people's contexts, serving other people's intentions" (pp. 293–294).

While traditional accounts locate meaning within the minds of individuals, social semioticians recognize meaning construction as a socially and historically mediated process that draws on existing explanations of the world. Events occur quickly at the lower levels involving microscopic changes; time at the higher-level timescales extends across centuries involving large-scale changes that proceed gradually (i.e., the coming of the next ice age). Timescales are dimensions of an ecological system in which lower levels are constituent of the higher levels, with the higher levels involving conceptualizations and interpretations of processes and experiences at the lower levels. Human semiosis, meaning-making based on experience, involves interpretations of experiences that have been constructed and revisited over long periods of time as well as information from ongoing experiences.

Discourses, artifacts, and cultural models all operate within and across timescales. Discourses can reflect ways of speaking and interacting that connect to a favorite grandparent. Parents may remember particular artifacts including books, from their own youth. Cultural models are related to what types of books adolescents should read. Discourses, artifacts, and cultural models all involve histories that impact the ways people make sense of their worlds. All three of these constructs reach across multiple timescales as people use words, objects, and understandings across time to make sense of the present and to plan for the future. Throughout this sense-making process, people draw upon the recent past, familial stories, and larger social histories as they construct meanings of their worlds and themselves.

Lemke's timescales (2000) provide a tool for conceptualizing identity formation and other long-term processes including school trajectories and literacy learning. Identities do not change and develop based only on ongoing activity at shorter timescales. Identity relates to the "social types or categories we identify with on the basis of shared values" (Lemke, 2000, p. 283); identities involve experiences at historical and familial timescales, as well as historically constructed cultural models and dominant and alternative discourses.

- *Historical Timescales.* Historical timescales reference historic accounts of people and events that are known to participants with various degrees of specificity. While participants in my study did not recount textbook-style details of these histories, they brought general understandings that have been conveyed through the media, school experiences, family stories, and shared cultural knowledge. Not only were people recipients of these historical discourses, they were also actors within historicized contexts.

- *Familial Timescales.* Familial timescales reference the personal experiences of family members and the ways understandings of these experiences circulate within families. Familial timescales included accounts and discourses that supported, exposed, and challenged generally accepted understandings of the world.

Temporal ways of understanding the world extend beyond the here and now of ongoing experience. Lemke (2000) explained that "self-conscious personal identity" reflected what people "are inclined to believe or doubt, desire or dislike, expect or find surprising" (p. 283), which are always grounded in the social and in the past. Identities are never stable, singular, nor consistent, and people enact and embody multiple identities as they move across contexts and interact with different groups of people. Finally, the interactions people have with family members and close friends are particularly powerful and become "an essential part of who we are" (p. 285). Thus, the families within this project have huge effects on the ways students make sense of their experiences; literacy and schooling are deeply embedded in the nonschool experiences and understandings of students.

CONCLUSION

Time is intricately connected to learning, identities are assumed over time, institutional temporal policies relate to time, and humans are temporal beings who draw upon multiple timescales as they act and interact in daily life. In addition, schools and research initiatives bring their own temporal expectations to schooling. However, these dimensions of time have generally remained invisible in educational research and practices. Theoretical constructs such as timescales, discourses, artifacts, and cultural models all invoke time and enable researchers and educators to identify, explore, and begin to make sense of the school experiences of students. These theoretical tools allow us to conceptualize families as negotiating journeys rather than as occupying static spaces.

As Javon moved through school, temporal analysis allowed me to witness learning across time, explore ongoing identity construction relative to literacy, examine the intersection between Javon and the temporal expectations of schooling, and consider how Javon drew upon events at multiple timescales. Specifically, across time Javon negotiated the purposes of literacy, the types of books he enjoyed, and reading school-assigned texts. He explored identities in conjunction with his peers, as they traded R. L. Stine books, and with me as we discussed his initial participation in the project. Negotiations with school involved the challenge to read 25 books, being rushed through his work, and enduring hall sweeps. As he moved through school, Javon encountered teachers, such as Mr. Whitney, who drew on multiple dimensions of his own past as he worked with his students.

A short-term study might easily miss these changes and consistencies across time. Discourses—including ways of talking about schools and teachers, books, reader, and reading—occur across time. They often reflect established cultural models related to being a good student or a competent reader. A variety of artifacts, including books, circulate between home and school, among participants, and across time as participants operate in worlds that extend beyond the here and now referencing past experiences and possible futures. In the chapters that follow, I look across the 11 family cases to explore the ways students and their parents make sense of literacy, schooling, and identity across and within time.

CHAPTER 2

Time and Change

Although during the first two phases of the project, I did not attend explicitly to time, as I explained earlier, the markers of time were present. Being in 1st grade was linked to being 5 and 6 years old, but being 8 years old and in the 1st grade was considered as a problem. Time was invoked when I considered the school's placement on the state list of schools that needed to improve and the foreboding timetable for closure if student achievement did not improve by the end of the school year. Although I did not recognize or attend to time as a contextual factor in students' lives, multiple manifestations of time were always present in the data set. In contrast, when I described the school, classroom, and neighborhood context, descriptions of physical spaces predominated. Adam (2008) described time as the "invisible temporal" (p. 7), explaining that "matter in space is visible; processes are not" (p. 10). Processes always involve time, but time itself is often invisible. As the project continued over 8 years, time became increasingly visible.

Once I began to recognize time, multiple temporal dimensions became apparent, and time manifested itself in a myriad of ways. Family members drew upon their past experiences, schools measured student progress in relation to temporal benchmarks, children and parents looked forward to possible futures, and family stories were told and retold across the project. The longitudinal data set provided clues about how "identities are formed, maintained, discarded or reworked over time" (Adam, 2008, p. 10).

Saldaña (2003) argued that longitudinal research was uniquely suited to documenting change over time. In reference to his own longitudinal qualitative research, he maintained that researchers could not think about time without considering change, nor could they conceptualize change without implicating time. Longitudinal research allows researchers to attend to multiple and possible types of change. Saldaña (2003) described the context in which events occur as an ever-changing "ocean" rather than a static "landscape" (p. 5). While time references change, time can also reference stability, and there can be no discussion of change without attention to what remains the same.

Longitudinal studies draw attention to patterns of change or stasis that are generally invisible in short-term studies. While shorter projects might present families, neighborhoods, and schools as static, longitudinal studies reveal change and remind us that there are no quintessential urban families, neighborhoods, or schools. Contexts are continually shifting, and both opportunities and challenges are continually appearing. Over time, student interests, reading practices, identities as readers, relationships with teachers, and expectations for the future are constantly evolving. Longitudinal research also makes visible both the recurrence of structural challenges and acts of agency on the part of participants as they voice alternative discourses and push back on structures and policies.

Saldaña (2003) argued that change was a particularly difficult concept to define because what constituted change in research studies was inextricably bonded with particular research contexts and the questions that were asked. In education, there are many words that denote change (e.g., *development, process, modification, transformation, trajectory*); however, documenting change over long periods of time can be challenging. As Pettigrew (1995) explained, the task of the longitudinal researcher is to "explore the complex, haphazard, and often contradictory ways that change emerges" (p. 93). The "slippery" (Saldaña, 2003, p. 8) and idiosyncratic nature of change means that it manifests itself differently in every study and that it is these unique manifestations that become visible through longitudinal research.

In this chapter, I use data from my longitudinal project to focus on changes I witnessed within neighborhoods, families, and schools as my former students moved into middle school. While it is traditional for researchers to situate their studies within physical settings, I situate my work within time and in relation to changes in people's lives. Throughout the 8-year project, most families continued to reside in low-income neighborhoods in the same city. However, notable changes occurred in families—some were related to their economic situations; others involved siblings growing older, moving out, and attending college. While some of these changes were expected (i.e., older siblings graduating from high school), others are unexpected and sometimes traumatic (i.e., difficulties with the law, death, illness). Changes for the focal students were often related to the transition into middle school; these changes involved challenges for students in school and with peers.

At the most basic and biological level, I marveled at the physical changes that had occurred in my former students. When we reunited, all of my former 6-year-olds towered over my 5-foot frame. They laughed as they stood beside me and compared our respective heights. They were no longer focused on Power Rangers and hand clapping rhymes. They spoke of girlfriends, getting their driver's licenses, and the various cliques at school. I often found myself marveling at their new heights and enacting cultural norms that included commenting on how much they had grown—an expected discourse that accompanies encountering children who have not been seen in a while. Their parents lamented the challenges of raising adolescents and spoke extensively about when they were young. We found ourselves commiserating about how quickly time passed.

Almost 50 years before the writing of this book, the community where most of the families continued to live had been the site of racial riots. African American residents were frustrated by unequal opportunities for jobs, education, and housing as well as tense relations with law enforcement agencies. The housing projects that currently surround the school where I taught 1st grade were built in the years following the riots as part of an initiative designed to address racial injustice. I began teaching at Rosa Parks Elementary School in 1988 and was shocked to discover that while the school served over 1,000 children, fewer than 10 White students were attending the school. Since then, the community surrounding Rosa Parks School has changed very little. Few businesses operate in the community, although a fast-food restaurant and a grocery store have opened in recent years.

CHANGING PLACES, MOVING HOMES

By middle school, all but one of the students had moved at least once since 1st grade (see Figure 2.1). With the exception of Angela, all of the students continued to attend schools in the same school district and reside in low-income areas of the city. Most families rented a series of apartments within a 5-mile radius of the elementary school where I used to teach.

While teachers and school administrators often identified mobility as a problem, mobility represented possibilities for families and was described by parents as an act of agency. Discourses that distinguished between quiet and noisy communities were often used. Desirable new apartments were described as quiet in terms of both noise and activity. After Ms. Horner moved into her mother's home, she reported, "It's very nice. Very quiet." Similarly, Ms.

Figure 2.1: Family Mobility

Christy	3 moves; included moving into foster mother's residence
Peter	3 moves; included moving in with his father
Bradford	2 moves
David	2 moves
Jermaine	2 moves
Alicia	1 move
Angela	1 move
Javon	1 move
Marvin	Did not move

Holt explained that despite being on a busy street, her new apartment was "nice and quiet." She reported that her former neighborhood, "got [to be] too much" and "a lot of things happen[ed] on May Road." She worried, "My boys are getting bigger and they [be] wanting to do things." She explained that there were adults in the neighborhood doing things that she could not condone; she would tell her boys, "'Nope, you can't do those [things],' so I got to move them away from them so I don't have to worry about it."

Similarly, Ms. Burns described her city neighborhood as "loud" and noted that this was why they were planning to move to the suburbs. Unlike other participants, Mr. and Ms. Burns both had associate degrees in business, and family resources that they could draw upon. In addition, Mr. Burns's health had improved, and his self-taught computer skills provided him with access to a good-paying job. They were also the only White family in the sample. Regarding the anticipated move, Ms. Burns explained:

> [It's the] Music. [The] people in general. There's not parties per se but you sit in the front room to try to watch a TV show and they've got their car doors open playing the radio as loud as they can so you can't hear your TV show. Or whatever. I mean you just can't enjoy your yard.

After moving to their new home, Ms. Burns spoke enthusiastically about their neighborhood in the suburbs, "It's not a lot of noises" and "just a whole different atmosphere out here."

Participants also referenced the stability of neighborhoods. Ms. Johnson explained with pride that one of her neighbors has lived in his house "all his life." Christy's foster mother, Ms. Robins, who has been living in the same home for over 15 years, explained that most of her neighbors had been in the neighborhood longer than she had. She remarked that the majority owned their own homes, which she identified as another indication of a good neighborhood.

Marvin's family was the only family in the sample that did not move during the 8-year project; they had lived in the same apartment for 10 years before the project started. While in the past Mr. Sherwood, Marvin's step-grandfather, was satisfied with the neighborhood and reported that it was "peaceful at night," at our final interview he reported that Marvin had been jumped earlier in the year and worried that there were more older kids hanging around on the street.

Drawing on cultural models that characterize urban and suburban communities, parents spoke of the benefits of living in the suburbs and attending suburban schools. Ms. Mason considered having Jermaine live with his aunt so that he could attend a suburban school. While Jermaine agreed that, "they teach you good [in the suburbs]," he remained concerned. "They got a lot of White kids. I don't want to be the only Black person going in that one school." Ms. Rodriguez thought that students in suburban schools generally did better with learning to read due to "better teachers, better books, better surroundings." Her son Leon, who had recently graduated from high school agreed, "They got better schools." Over the course of the research project most families discussed the possibility of moving into suburban neighborhoods. While some of the participants, like Jermaine, expressed concerns about attending schools that were primarily attended by White students, most of the parents believed that attending suburban schools would benefit their children. Only Angela's family had the financial resources to actually move into a suburban neighborhood.

In Peter's case, moving was traumatic. In 8th grade, his family moved to New York City. While Peter attended a magnet school that he liked, he got into fights on the way home from school everyday. As he explained, there was "another school down the street from our school and they started trouble most of the time." To avoid being jumped on the way home, Peter stopped going to school. As Ms. Horner explained, his grades "went just downhill. Couldn't believe it at all. I've never seen Peter do so, so bad." Although before moving to New York Peter consistently earned As and Bs, he never regained those grades maintaining only a B/C average when he returned to the research city.

The parents dreamt about and pursued quieter and more stable communities in which to raise their families. While moving was described by parents as an act of agency and possibility, months after moving to a new apartment in a new neighborhood, most families discovered that the new apartments they could afford were in neighborhoods that were no better than the places they had left, and they were again seeking new residences. Thus the parents' attempts to improve their families' living situations were generally thwarted.

Finally, neighborhoods marked differences between families and teachers. Unlike the teachers described by Ladson-Billings (1994), most of the teachers in this school district did not have social networks that linked them to the school community, nor did they live in the city. Only one teacher at Rosa Parks Elementary School lived in the school community. The rest of us drove into the city each day from our suburban residences. As Ms. Holt explained, not living in the school community had effects. She drew upon cultural models that characterize inner city communities, explaining that teachers "need to understand [the] children of this city." I minimally edited her words to construct the following connected account:

Because a lot of teachers don't live around the kids in the inner city so they don't know. They don't go through this every day. They don't. They

[are] there [in the community] from what? 8:00 [or] 7:30 to 3:30? They [are] inside the school. They don't come outside. (Ms. Holt chuckled as she spoke.) You don't even know what goes on outside of your school, you know? Even though you're working there, you should be putting yourself out there for those kids. I've never seen a teacher walk to the corner store in the city . . . which they should do. I'm not saying you should do it, but I'm just saying this way you kind of know what these children that you're dealing with *are* going through everyday.

Neighborhoods and residences marked differences that separated teachers from families. Keeping children safe, providing them with good schools, and living in stable communities were important goals of the parents. Unfortunately, with the exception of Angela, the new neighborhoods families could afford shared the same challenges as the neighborhoods they had left behind and did not lead to the possibilities parents had imagined for their children. Despite significant changes in residences and communities, much remained the same for the families.

CHANGING FAMILIES

Changes also occurred within families. When I started the project, the parents were raising 6-year-olds. By the end of the project, the students were in middle school and their parents were raising adolescents. All but one of the parents had become grandparents. Not only did the student participants grow, but their siblings also grew up during the 8-year project. Several siblings, including three of Alicia's older brothers, three of Bradford's older siblings, four of David's siblings, and two of Javon's older siblings graduated from high school. In at least five families, older siblings attended some college. Two older siblings—Bradford's brother and Jermaine's sister—eventually graduated with 4-year degrees.

Other siblings did not fare as well. Marvin's sister dropped out of high school as did Javon's older brother. These situations were extremely stressful for both families. When Javon's brother was arrested, his mother sent him down south to live with an aunt in order to get him away from friends who were headed in the wrong direction. As Ms. Mason reported, he "turned his life around." Marvin's sister met an older man when she was 14 and dropped out of high school. While he was still distraught by the situation, Mr. Sherwood explained that things were somewhat better now:

She's safe you know. She had some incidents and stuff like that in the past . . . fights, stuff like that happens in life but, but she's maintaining.

We miss her, you know, but nothing that we can do. She had to do it. She out there you know, that was a strain. But she's doing okay.

Most of the older siblings were working at jobs that their parents described as temporary (i.e., sanitation workers, factory employees, maintenance workers, construction workers, day care workers). In two cases, siblings seemed to be making career gains; Jermaine's older sister had become a school nurse, and Bradford's older brother was in college and headed for a career as a tennis pro. Both the successes and the struggles of older siblings affected my former students—suggesting possibilities and dangers.

As older siblings grew up, the number of people living in households generally decreased (see Figure 2.2). This was true of all the families except for Christy's, Peter's, and Angela's. Christy and her sister had spent the last few years of the project in a foster family after they had been removed from their mother's home; at the end of 8th grade she and her sister were in the process of being legally adopted. They joined a family that included a biological daughter, other adopted children, and another foster child who was also adopted. Peter had moved in with his father, his stepmother, and half siblings; he later relocated to his grandmother's house. There were no changes in Angela's family.

At the beginning of the research project, the participants and I were parents raising children; by the time my former students were in grades 7 and 8, many of us had become, or were expecting to become grandparents (see Figure 2.3). Mr. Sherwood and his wife Doris, who had raised their grandchildren, were now great grandparents. Only Ms. Horner and Ms. Burns were not yet grandparents; notably neither Peter nor Angela had older siblings.

Figure 2.2: Changes in Family Size

	People in the Household	
	Grade 1	*Grade 8*
Ms. Johnson (David)	8	5
Ms. Mason (Javon)	8	4
Ms. Rodriguez (Alicia)	8	4
Ms. Holt (Bradford)	7	3
Ms. Burns (Angela)	4	4
Ms. Hudson (Jermaine)	4	3
Mr. Sherwood (Marvin)	4	3
Ms. Denver (Christy)	3	6
Ms. Horner (Peter)	3	6

Figure 2.3: Grandchildren in the Families

Mr. Sherwood (Marvin)	Several grandchildren
	Two great grandchildren
Ms. Johnson (David)	Five grandchildren
Ms. Denver (Christy; adopted mother)	Two grandchildren
Ms. Lilly (researcher)	Two grandchildren
Ms. Mason (Jermaine)	Two grandchildren
Ms. Hudson (Jermaine)	One grandchild
Ms. Rodriguez (Alicia)	One grandchild
Ms. Holt (Bradford)	First grandchild was expected
Ms. Burns (Angela)	No grandchildren
Ms. Horner (Peter)	No grandchildren

Other changes occurred as well. Ms. Horner married and had a baby daughter, but eventually left her husband. Ms. Rodriguez was dating a man whom she would eventually marry.

Families also changed due to death and illness. David's father had died the summer after he was in my 1st-grade class. Christy had lost contact with her stepfather who died in another state sometime between the time Christy was in grades 5 and 8. Marvin and Alicia were in 8th grade when Mr. Sherwood's twin brother passed away, and Ms. Rodriguez's father died of cancer. Ms. Burns struggled with carpel tunnel syndrome, and Ms. Holt had recently recovered completely from back surgery, but was struggling to recover from a taxing bout of walking pneumonia, during which she lost 35 pounds. In some cases, the physical struggles faced by families were complicated by a lack of adequate health care, made evident as parents described trips to the emergency room because chronic problems remained unaddressed, or long periods of time waiting to obtain what should have been routine medical procedures. Perhaps most concerning were the ongoing difficulties Ms. Green, Christy's mom, faced with bipolar disorder. She was eventually institutionalized in another state and diagnosed with HIV/AIDS. Christy often spoke of her mother and shared with me the cards and letters her mother had sent.

Changes in families carried meanings that informed the ways my former students and their family members made sense of experience. The familial timescale was especially powerful as stories were told and retold, experiences were interpreted, and shared meanings were constructed. Changes within families were not merely series of events; they were markers of trajectories characterized by possibilities and disappointments. When older siblings graduated from high school, possibilities were raised. When parents received substandard health care, challenges, obstacles, and inequities were revealed.

CHANGING SCHOOLS

The transition to middle school was difficult for some of the students. Middle school brought new schedules, changing classes and teachers, lockers, longer bus rides, and new friends. Parents drew upon cultural models related to middle school as they noted the challenges faced by their children.

> *Ms. Hudson*: He's [Jermaine's] used to having just one
>   teacher . . . not going to all these different classes.
> *Ms. Burns*: They are more responsible for their own work . . . instead
>   of having your teacher hand you a piece of paper and saying this
>   is your homework, now it's they might write it on the board and
>   say read these pages and answer these questions so they have
>   to make sure they write their assignments down and do them.
> *Ms. Johnson*: [It's] very different, going to all the different
>   classes, you know, he says you know with the work [getting
>   harder] and everything being more, it's a challenge.
> *Ms. Robins*: Middle school is more homework.
> *Mr. Sherwood*: [Marvin] can't handle the people when he talk
>   to them, and they try to tell him [what to do], they say
>   you can't do this and you can't do that. . . . You know
>   you got to be following the rules and stuff like that.
> *Ms. Mason*: When they got in middle school, they had to walk.
>   Cause elementary, the elementary kids at least they get a
>   chance to ride the bus if they live too far away. . . . And I
>   think [for] my kids their work is getting a little harder.

Middle school also brought new temporal expectations. Some children and parents reported that the pace of instruction had increased and that keeping up in class was sometimes difficult. Jermaine described himself and most of his peers as needing more time than the so-called smart kids:

> When they teach you so fast, you don't pick up that fast. They say they
> do like a week of this and then next week we do another one. [Then
> they] do something that's different . . . . 'Cause I don't pick up stuff fast
> like the other kids. I feel like there's only two smart kids in my class and
> they pick up stuff like that. But we don't. I don't pick up stuff that fast.

While Jermaine focused on his own abilities and argued that his teachers needed to slow down to accommodate him and his peers, Angela contrasted reading assignments in middle school with those in elementary school. In elementary school teachers did not generally assign specific books; Angela was simply asked to read for 20 minutes each night. Angela's mother explained that when Angela "hit middle school, they threw a book at you and said 'read.'" As Angela explained she had to read "certain chapters and pages" to complete assignments that were due on designated dates.

In addition to increased expectations of children and the faster pace of instruction, several parents mentioned the challenges of adolescence including relationships with peers:

> *Ms. Holt*: He [Bradford] started getting into it with
> [other kids], it seem like the kids in the neighborhood
> would take neighborhood things to school.
> *James* (Alicia's Brother): Kids are older; [they] talk
> more. Kids have problems as they get older.
> *Mr. Sherwood*: Kids like to play and stuff like that you know in
> school. This and then he get involved but he end
> up getting um, then he end up getting um blamed
> for this and blamed for that you know.
> *Ms. Rodriguez*: You know and I know with her [Alicia's]
> hormones are going and thinking about the boys and all that.

Participants described the challenges of growing up and the social pressures students experienced—peer pressure, the problems faced by adolescents, and an increasing fascination with the opposite sex all contributed to new types of challenges.

Finally, some participants identified teachers as contributing to the challenges faced by children in school. One of the most often repeated changes was that teachers did not care about their students. As Jermaine reported, "They just want the money. They're not trying to teach you." Ms. Sherwood, drawing on cultural models often imposed on poor urban students, worried that teachers were often not prepared for the challenges they faced in middle schools:

> Some of them [teachers] never figure it out. The first thing coming out of their mind is that the child is there, "They [the children] don't have no respect, they nasty, talk nasty, I'm just going to kick them out." And that's it. And that's not good for the child. That's not good for the child. I hate for a child to be out of school. It breaks my heart to see a child out of school.

Ms. Rodriguez worried that teachers were often unreasonable in their expectations. She remembered a time when her son, Tyreek, got in trouble. "[The] teacher called me because he was laughing. I'm like, 'Don't *you* laugh?' That don't make sense. 'Well, he was interrupting the classroom.' 'Okay? But don't *you* laugh?' I was [really annoyed], see they call you for the most silliest things."

Despite these challenges, there were also highlights, special teachers, and fondly recalled events and activities for some of the students. Peter attended a higher achievement program over the summer at a local Catholic school. As his mother explained, he received a certificate and had been invited back to the program the following year although he was unable to attend due to moving to New York. David was still talking about his 4th-grade class trip to a farm in Massachusetts. Marvin and Angela spent the summer after 8th grade participating in a summer reading clinic that I directed at a local college. When Marvin did his presentation on banana slugs at the end of the clinic, it was the only time I had ever met his biological mother and father. In addition, almost all of the students recalled favorite teachers, fondly remembered experiences, and engaging activities.

CONCLUSION

Change was a constant in the accounts of my former students. New homes, changing families, new schools with new expectations, and memorable events contributed to the longitudinal accounts I present. In many cases the changes outlined above were decidedly problematic. Low incomes resulted in families struggling to find safe and quiet neighborhoods, obtain quality health care, and achieve access to high quality schools. While high school graduations, college admittances, marriages, and the birth of babies were celebrated, a few families struggled with children leaving school and sometimes experiencing run-ins with the law. In addition, my former students had recently transitioned into middle school, where they attended overcrowded and underfunded schools that often failed to meet the needs of students. While many of the students fondly recalled some school experiences, these experiences were generally short-lived and had little effect on their long-term trajectories.

The families of my former students were remarkably and simultaneously agentive and vulnerable. Parents and students actively sought better places to raise their children, but generally lacked financial resources that provided access to these better resourced communities. Family members supported each other by making sense of experiences in ways that suggested possibilities and hope, but sometimes those possibilities shattered as children left school and experienced negative encounters with the law. Some children attended high quality educational programs and benefited from the time they spent in these programs, but their families often lacked the means to sustain participation over time. Agency was apparent in the commitment of parents to provide children with safe housing and positive school experiences, yet limited by the structural constraints that accompanied living in a low-income community and attending underfunded schools.

A challenge in this project was to capture the changes in the lives of my former students and their families, as well as the evolving identities and meanings that accompanied the events of their lives. I crafted a set of methodologies that included tracking discourses across time and exploring accounts that recurred in the data set. I have also identified and named some of the cultural models that people accessed across time. (See Appendix B for the methodological details about my study.) In the chapter that follows, I focus specifically on artifacts—in this case texts—that appeared and reappeared in the data set.

CHAPTER 3

Students, Reading, and Books

Books are among the artifacts of schooling. Every book has a history and often a reputation. Books carry cultural messages into classrooms. Some books have been used in classrooms over long periods of time, they have historically constructed meanings—meanings about the types of people who read these books. Newer books also carry social messages—books that have been made into popular movies often carry social value among peers. Likewise, books that depict situations or address issues that are considered inappropriate for school can act as markers of resistance. Some books reference multiple historical timescales. Reading *Moby Dick* or *A Tale of Two Cities* is not just temporal due to their references to colonial America or the French Revolution; these books carry meanings as educational texts and occupy a place in the traditional literary cannon. Familial timescales are invoked when parents remember the books they read in high school.

In classrooms, the books of the past coexist with artifacts and interactions in the present. These historical remixes contribute to environments in which students claim or reject particular texts as they define themselves as particular types of readers. In this chapter, I explore some of the meanings that students attribute to texts including schoolbooks, series books, the media, and magazines. I examine the discourses and cultural models that students draw upon as they talk about books and themselves as readers. I close by examining the ways children's textual preferences relate to reading practices in their homes.

When I asked my 1st-grade students about what they read, I assumed they would describe particular types of books (i.e., funny stories, books about animals). Instead, the 6-year-olds generally responded as if I were asking a rather silly question and provided logical answers saying they read "words," "signs," "books," and "boxes." When the children offered book titles, they generally listed books from our classroom library. Only two children mentioned book titles from home—both were Disney versions of fairy tales.

By grades 4 and 5, the children expressed wide-ranging reading preferences. Alicia reported reading books from *The Baby-sitter's Club* (Martin & Lerangris, 1986–2000), *Winnie the Pooh* books (staff writers, 1966–current),

Goosebumps books (Stine, 1992–1997), a biography of Dr. Martin Luther King, and a biography of a popular basketball star. Jermaine enjoyed books about animals, tornados, *Blues Clues* (staff writers, 1999–current), and *Clifford the Big Red Dog* (Bridwell, 1963–current). Christy identified chapter books, the *Arthur* Series (Brown, 1982–current), and *The Kid in the Red Jacket* (Park, 1988), a book she had been assigned to read in school. In grades 4 and 5, schoolbooks were no longer predominant and only two children mentioned books that were assigned at school. Students' book preferences revealed variety in genre and reading difficulty, ranging from children's books to young adult biographies. As reported by other researchers (Davila & Patrick, 2010), some children appeared less enthusiastic about reading as they moved from grade 5 into middle school.

BOOK PREFERENCES IN MIDDLE SCHOOL

By middle school, the students' reading preferences had sedimented and most students identified favorite genres, books, or authors:

Jermaine: [Only] one book [I am interested in], *Frederick Douglass Fights for Freedom* [Davidson, 1989]. . . It talk about how like Frederick Douglass . . . he wasn't in slavery. He lived with his grandma. They took him from his mom. He didn't have no home, and he was going from place to place telling people about his life.

Angela: I read this book in two days [shows me a book from the *Unfortunate Events* Series]. I love these. All the books are [written] to Beatrice. It's fun.

David: It's [*Goosebumps* is] kind of like spooky and adventurous. So when you're finding out what's going on, there's still something you need to [understand] for what's happening. And you think you know what's going on in the book, what's really happening, it makes you wait a little longer.

Alicia: I like to read love stories . . . it's a story called something about virgins and I got that [from] the lady that's next door.

Peter: I'm really into like *Lord of the Rings*. I have all the games, I have the Monopoly. . . it has like all the properties, all the places from *Lord of the Rings*.

These quotes are filled with statements of affiliation—"I love these," "I'm really into," and "only one book." Unlike earlier accounts, middle school readers identified specific books, authors, series, and genres, and no longer voiced generic references to words and books.

As students became clearer about the types of books they enjoyed, they also became adamant about what they did not like.

> *Jermaine*: Stuff that has too much history, too much information.
>   Like that (pointed to a history textbook that was sitting nearby).
> *Christy*: [I don't like] mysteries. I don't want to go through all
>   that . . . [And I don't like] this book we read in English. . . .
>   *To Kill a Mockingbird*. It's boring. I ain't getting into it yet.

Jermaine pointed to his history textbook, and Christy named a title that was a staple in the literary cannon for American high school students. Both described reading these books as dreary and tedious. In general, students disliked reading books that they felt were too complex—"too much history" or "too much information"; as Christy reported in reference to reading mysteries, I don't "want to go through all that." Their voices reflected cultural models of reading that characterize reading as tedious, solitary, and sedentary.

As documented by literacy scholars (Ivey & Broaddus, 2001; Worthy, Moorman, & Turner, 1999), adolescents often identify historical texts as less engaging than other types of texts. Worthy and her colleagues (1999) found that middle school students ranked informational books near the bottom of a list of 20 genres (18th out of 20 genres). These historical texts were ranked above only encyclopedias and information books about math and science. Ivey and Broaddus (2001) explained that school reading lists often featured award winning realistic and historical fiction texts while only 1% of students identified these as the "best" texts they read at home and only 2% of students identified these as the "best" texts they read at school. Kimmel (1982) argues that we are witnessing an "emergence of children's books for adults" (p. 41), and notes that "knowing about literature is one thing; knowing about children, quite another" (p. 42). In other words, Kimmel worries that what adults identify as high quality literature may not include the books that students love.

In addition to historical texts, my former students identified other books that they did not enjoy reading.

> *Marvin*: [I don't like] those books, you got those little
>   books I don't know what you call them. You got to
>   read them. They got little sections inside that you got
>   to read [He is describing his ELA anthology].
> *David*: [I don't like] some stories that um, that just give
>   the answer early you know. What's going on early

in the story so then you could figure out the book
ending. You don't want to read it no more.

Peter: [I don't like] kiddy books. I don't like them, my sister
makes me read them to her. My sister [is] at my dad's
house. She has like these little miniature books
that I read to her—like Disney books.

Jermaine: [I don't] like science books. Like in the library
how you have the space stuff. I don't like to read
that. I don't like to really read romance books.

Angela: [The social studies textbook is] boring, too much
information. In one ear and out the other.

Students enacted identity positions through the textual artifacts they
chose. In general students distanced themselves from books that were assigned reading. Jermaine disliked his history textbook and the science books
he found in the school library. Marvin and Angela critiqued their English
Language Arts anthology and social studies textbooks. In each case, students presented themselves as being forced to read books (e.g., "you got to
read them") and distanced themselves from school texts through spoken or
implied identity statements (i.e., "I don't like. . . ."). While not required by
his teachers, Peter complained about the kiddie books that his sister would
"make" him read. As reported by Miller (2010), choice was particularly important to the students. In addition to their dismissal of schoolbooks, some
students rejected other books. Jermaine clearly disliked romances. Cultural
models of self—related to gender and maturity—were invoked as students
positioned themselves as certain types of readers.

By middle school, students' reading preferences were fairly intractable
despite efforts by teachers and parents to expand students' reading interests. Based on her interest in African American history and Jermaine's interest in Frederick Douglass, Ms. Hudson reported subscribing to a history
magazine for Jermaine, "[I] ordered that magazine just especially for him
to look through." When the magazine arrived Jermaine asked his mother,
"What I'm going to look at this for?" Jermaine dismissed the possibility
that he might be interested in the magazine. In a second example, Ms. Holt
explained that Bradford was not interested in reading a book about Martin
Luther King that he was assigned to read in school. As she explained:

I have no idea what he did with that book. I have no idea. It didn't
interest him. He said "I'm not trying to read it. I already been through
that damn book." I figure if you gave him a soccer book or a baseball
book [then he would read it].

She argued that the teacher should:

> Give him something that he enjoys doing and he'll read it. You give him
> this book about these little animals and all this stuff, he's not interested
> in animals. He's afraid of most of them. Why you want to have him read
> about something he's afraid of?

Mr. Sherwood makes a similar point about his grandson, Marvin:

> He'll get into that [pointing to the local section of the newspaper] but
> he won't get into nothing like that [shows me the other sections of the
> paper]. Not even those sports you know, he won't read that type of
> stuff. Where he's looking at [is] advertising [to] see if he can jumpstart
> [his Grandmother] on [buying] stuff. [He's] like "give me this and give
> me that."

The students in this sample had very different interests. Jermaine enjoyed reading about Frederick Douglass, while Bradford destroyed a book
about Martin Luther King. Ms. Holt suspects that Bradford would be interested in reading about sports, while Marvin was not. The texts that students
chose to read or not read were enactments of identity and had consequences
relative to social status.

While many of the students complained about the books they were assigned to read in school, they also encountered books that they loved:

> *Jermaine*: Listen, I had read *Maniac Magee, Freak the*
> *Mighty,* and there's a *Max the Mighty.* That's the books
> I read at school. Mmm-hmm. They're good.
> *David*: There was one book I didn't miss [class for]. That
> was *Call of the Wild.* That was a good book.
> *Peter*: I like the books like *Sounder* and *Holes.* I just finished reading
> *Scorpions.* When I was in New York actually I read it for my
> own and then when I came here I had to read it for school.
> *Javon*: [I'd read other books by Walter Dean Myers] if I could find
> some.
> *Angela*: *Holes* was a good book, but it started off slow. *Holes*
> was [assigned] last year. It was a really good book.

With the exception of the *Call of the Wild* (London, 1903), there is
some consistency in the types of schoolbooks that the students enjoyed.
These books all featured male protagonists in contemporary situations. All
of the books were published after 1983. Most students were not interested

in classic pieces of literature; these books draw on established cultural models about quality literature (e.g., serious themes, historical significance, complex characters) that define them as worthy of school attention. Unfortunately, these books often deal with content that is unfamiliar to students. Ladson-Billings (2009) noted that these texts are inaccessible and irrelevant to many students, at least in part because they were originally written for adults and explore adult themes. She warned that this may be a particular problem for African American children who may have little in common with the types of experiences presented in these texts.

In addition, expressing an enjoyment of classic literature requires particular types of identity commitments that many students did not make during the interviews. For example, David was one of the few children in the study who spoke enthusiastically about classic texts. This positioning as a reader was consistent with David's school identity. He was on the honor role, got good grades in his classes, liked his teachers, and loved his school. To David, reading classic texts was one dimension of the cultural model that accompanied being a "good student" and connected him to his ultimate dream—"Get a job, keep it steady, to get a nice house . . . get her [his mom] a nice car, stay loyal, stay respectful." However, for other students, being a reader of classic literature was less attractive and referenced being a bookworm or nerd—positionings that are often negatively portrayed on television and in movies.

Some students disliked the books that their teachers read aloud in the class. As Alicia explained:

Alicia: It's ["The Tell-Tale Heart's"] kinda boring.
CCL: Yeah? Do you think it's scary?
Alicia: No, it ain't scary.
CCL: (laughs) Why did you say it's boring?
　　What about it's kinda annoying?
Alicia: 'Cause, it's just, I think the story ain't boring, I just think [it's] the way my teacher reads it. So that makes it boring.

In a similar vein, Christy reported that *To Kill a Mockingbird* (Lee, 1960/2002) was boring, "We read that *To Kill a Mockingbird* together. The teacher read it to us and we followed along." Listening to the teacher read, involved passivity and reception rather than enactment and investment. While reading the texts individually might have provided some students with opportunities to interact with the texts and view themselves as readers of those texts, hearing texts read aloud reinforced distances between the texts and students' lives contributing to the sense that the texts were imposed on students. Ms. Holt associated reading with being sedentary, "I'd never even think about reading a book that thick. With a thousands of pages, I mean they'd [her children would have to] just sit hours and hours and just read. Bradford sit that still that long? I guess he can't sit still that long." Emig (1977) challenges this cultural model of reading as passive and sedentary, as she draws on the work of Rosenblatt (1994) to argue "the connotation of passivity too often accompanies the notion of receptivity when reading" (p. 123). Rosenblatt's transactional approach highlighted the active role that readers play in making meaning as they read. As she maintains, "the reader needs to slough off the old self-image as passively receiving the electric shocks of the verbal stimuli" (Rosenblatt, 1994, p. 132).

READING SERIES BOOKS

Series books are big business (Greenlee, Monson, & Taylor, 1996; Saltman, 1997) and have been highly marketable for a very long time. While dime novels began to appear in the 1860s (Ross, 1995), today's readers are probably more familiar with *The Bobbsey Twins* (Hope, 1904–1979), *Anne of Green Gables* (Montgomery, 1908), *The Hardy Boys* (Dixon, 1927–current), and *Nancy Drew* (Keene, 1930–current)—series books that have been read by recent generations (Greenlee, Monson, & Taylor, 1996; Mackey, 1990). These books characteristically involve exciting quick moving and predictable plots with youthful protagonists who solve problems without the assistance of adults (Reid & Cline, 1997).

Although popular, series books are also controversial. Saltman (1997) worried that bookstores, classrooms, and libraries were "groaning under the weight of children's series" (p. 23). She wondered "If children read predominately formula [books], do they lose forever the opportunity of meeting, at the most appropriate and potent developmental moment, stories designed not with entertainment, but with unforgettable characters, gripping plots, rich themes, and powerful language" (p. 24).

Ross (1995) reported that when she was a child, "Teachers did not count series books as 'real books,' while librarians justified their refusal to stock *The Bobbsey Twins* by claiming series books to be proven enemies of good reading" (p. 203). Worthy, Moorman, and Turner (1999) noted that teachers tended to prefer "young adult novels" and felt pressured to provide children with high quality literature in classrooms. While some teachers felt that series books were useful because they kept some kids reading, fewer than a third of the classrooms visited by Worthy and her colleagues (1999) provided more than a few copies of these books demonstrating an "ever-increasing gap between student preferences and the materials that schools provide and recommend" (p. 23). They noted that school library budgets were often tight resulting in the acquisition of small numbers of books and that the most popular books were perennially unavailable due to high demand. Like the students described by Kimmel (1982) and Hall and Coles (1999), the books loved by students were often not the same books appreciated by teachers.

Even in grade 1, series books, including the *Arthur* Series (Brown, 1982–current) and *Clifford the Big Red Dog* Series (Bridwell, 1963–current), were popular with the children. By middle school series books were clearly the most popular type of books. Notable series include *Goosebumps* (Stine, 1992–1997), *The Baby-sitter's Club* Series (Martin & Lerangris, 1986–2000) and the *Harry Potter* Series (Rowling, 1997–2007). Reflecting findings from several studies (Davila & Patrick, 2010; Ujiie & Krashen, 2002; Worthy et al., 1999), books by R. L. Stine were the most popular. Six out of the nine students, five boys and Alicia (who had four older brothers who had also read the *Goosebumps* books), mentioned *Goosebumps* when I asked them what they liked to read. David had read five or six books from the *Goosebumps* Series; Peter had read these books when he was younger but had moved on to *The Lord of the Rings* Series (Tolkien, 1954–1955). Two of the three girls reported reading books from *The Baby-sitter's Club* Series. Despite most of these series' being written at a 4th/5th grade level and considered easy reading for students in middle school, my students continued to read these books. Alicia had read over 20 books from *The Baby-sitter's Club* Series, "I used to read Baby-sitter's Club at elementary school. Now I read them in middle school." She assured me that she never got tired of them. Christy reported that she only owned one *Baby-sitter's Club* book, but has read several at school.

Several researchers and educators (Feitelson, Kita, & Goldstein, 1986; Ross, 1995; Worthy, 1996) note that series books are particularly attractive to children who struggle with reading. As Worthy (1996) argues, series books "provide readers with a sense of mastery over the conventions of reading" (p. 210). Over time as the children read multiple books in a series, the characters, language, and content of the books become increasingly familiar, enabling even children who struggle with reading to comprehend the predictable plots and thus experience reading as enjoyable and relatively effortless.

While the *Harry Potter* Series received accolades in the popular press for its impact on adolescent reading, its reviews from participants were mixed. Some students reported reading multiple books in the series, while other students found the texts overwhelming, unmanageable, or not compelling. Jermaine, who was reading at a 5th-grade reading level, described his experience with reading a *Harry Potter* book that had been assigned in middle school:

Jermaine: The last book I read—what was it? I think it was
     Harry Potter. That big one. I think it had 24 chapters.
CCL: You read the whole thing?
Jermaine: I didn't read the whole thing. I read like two or three
     chapters of it. It was long. It had itty bitty words. It was too much.
     [I] told my teacher I had to take that back [saying] "I'm not going
     to be able to finish that." Mostly everyone in my class read that
     book. So one boy, two, four of them didn't like [it] so they had got
     another book. I read the Harry Potter for awhile. It was too long.

With his teacher's permission, Jermaine chose a book from the *Goose-bumps* Series.

Access also affected students' interest in Harry Potter. Christy, who had recently been adopted by a single mother who was struggling financially to raise six foster and adopted children, did not have access to the first two books in the series; Christy started with the third book but never finished it. In contrast, Angela, a competent and avid reader, whose family had the financial means to relocate to a suburban community, had sequentially read the first five books. Mackey (1990) noted that series books are easily accessible for children whose families have the economic means to purchase books as they are released or as children move through the series. Other children often experience book series in piecemeal fashions—reading books out of sequence and relying on availability in libraries or classrooms.

More competent readers found the *Harry Potter* books to be engaging and compelling. Ms. Mason reported that "[Javon] was into *Harry Potter* books." She explained, "He had read all of them except for the last one that came out." She suspected that he had lost interest, explaining, "when the book first came out he kept saying he's going to buy the book. And [then] I noticed he got into the game system." Like his mother, Javon used the past tense to describe his Harry Potter interests saying "I *did* like to read Harry Potter." He reported that he was planning to read the next book in the series and identified J. K. Rowling as his favorite author, but did not sound as enthusiastic about the books as he had been in the past; as described earlier, Javon attributed his reduced interest in Harry Potter to the imposed goal of reading 25 books during the school year. In all, five of the nine students reported reading a *Harry Potter* book or part of a book, or their teacher reading sections of the books to the class. Only two students had actually completed at least one book in the series.

Some series books, including *Goosebumps* and *Harry Potter*, are often identified as being outside the purview of school—*Goosebumps* due to its focus on violence and horror, and *Harry Potter* for its attention to fantasy and black magic. Greenlee and her colleagues (1996) note the "sub-literary status" (p. 217) of series books, while Reid and Cline (1997) lament that they "still receive too little respect in schools and libraries" (p. 68). However, not all series books are equally scorned (Reid & Cline, 1997). Interestingly, the ways in which books deal with time is one of the variables that separates acceptable series books from nonacceptable books. Series books in which time passes and characters grow and change (e.g., Laura Ingalls Wilder's books, *Anne of Green Gables, Harry Potter* Series) have been treated more generously by critics, librarians, and educators than books in which characters never age or develop (e.g., *Nancy Drew, The Baby-sitter's Club, Goosebumps*) (Greenlee, Monson, & Taylor, 1996). Mackey (1990) refers to these books as ones that "constantly repeat an endless present" (p. 486). Other factors that contribute to the acceptability of series books include emphasizing values, family, collaboration, and integrity (Reid & Cline, 1997).

Despite their denials that their peers read books, some students described sharing series books with their peers or siblings. Peter shared *Goosebumps* and later *The Lord of the Rings* with his friends; Javon and Alicia shared *Goosebumps* with their siblings. Based on the popularity of these books, it appears that reading series books have social meanings that position these books as more palatable to students and more socially acceptable. As Saltman (1997) described, "There is a social glue, being able to dance the social dance with friends, which includes reading the same titles friends are reading and catching allusions to characters, mysteries, or gore" (p. 23). Reid and Cline (1997) noted that some students would carry particular books to class—in particular they favored the *Goosebumps* Series (Stine, 1992–1997). In contrast to reading classic literature, reading series books maintained a non-school affiliation that might better reflect identity positionings that students were comfortable assuming.

Overall, Mackey (1990) wondered if the youth orientation of these books created a community that was beyond the purview of adults. She asked whether there was "a kind of intellectual satisfaction in the reading of series books" (p. 487) that was overlooked or dismissed by adults. In a similar vein, Reid and Cline (1997) suggested that in some cases the reading of unacceptable authors, such as R. L. Stine, could be understood as acts of "reading rebellion" (p. 71). Reading particular types of texts reference cultural models of who is expected to read those texts and the types of people they are assumed to be.

THE MEDIA, TECHNOLOGY, AND READING PREFERENCES

Of the nine students I interviewed in middle school only two, Alicia and Angela, reported having Internet access in their homes. Alicia used the computer to chat with friends and visit websites. Angela's father was a self-taught and self-proclaimed computer geek. He had helped his daughters to construct their own websites on which Angela posted her artwork and authored a blog. Peter, David, Marvin, and Javon had working computers in their homes, but no Internet access. Jermaine and Bradford reported that their family computers were broken. Christy was the only child in the sample without a computer at home. A presentation by Jacobs (2009) noted that commercial e-mail and chatting were available in 1988. Texting was starting to gain popularity in 1992. Massively multiplayer online gaming was becoming common in 1997 and Google became an entity in 1998. By 2004, the time of this study, Internet access was common in middle-class homes. While most of the families in my study did own computers, only two could access the Internet at home, pointing to a significant technological gap. The students in my sample generally used their home computers to play games on CDs and spoke more about movies and game systems than they did about online literacy practices. Most did not report using e-mail or social networking sites.

Various scholars (Davila & Patrick, 2010; Krashen, 1993) note that youth tend to read books that have inspired popular films. This may be particularly true of struggling readers who can gain a sense of the story, become familiar with the characters, and be introduced to unfamiliar vocabulary by watching the movie which can support them as they read the text. In this study and as reported by Hall and Coles (1999), media practices affect students' reading preferences. However, it is essential that we recognize that these preferences are embedded in discourses and practices related to peer culture and popular entertainment, as well as the commercial interests that underlie these media ventures. The media brings a range of texts into the lives of students; some of these are strongly imposed. Despite being assigned by teachers, *Holes* (Sachar, 1998) was described as enjoyable by half of the students; they were in middle school when the movie was released. Three of the nine students reported that they had been assigned the book more than once during the past two years. As Peter reported, "Every year, I read *Holes* [in school]." Associations with the media, movies, and television were apparent in the students' reading preferences from first grade through middle school.

While the reading preferences of young children tended to reference television programs, particularly those on public broadcasting stations (e.g., *Arthur, Blue Clues, Clifford*), or movies produced by Disney (e.g., *The Lion King, Winnie the Pooh*), older students tended to identify popular movies. It is important to recognize that these are not simply personal preferences. These preferences are conceivably linked not only to the production industry and the advertising that surrounds these films but also to the ways these films are marketed to particular audiences, including young adolescents.

Carrying these books around and talking about them is an identity enactment that references popular texts of the present rather than "boring" books from the past. As Graff (2010) demonstrated in her study with young adolescent girls, the reading of particular texts can be used to "establish and maintain friendships" (p. 184). Graff explained that some books "were valued more for their subject matter and potential status as a cultural object than as objects to literally be read" (p. 184).

In some cases, technology and media practices and the relationships that students shared with peers around these books had social significance. Peter discussed and exchanged *The Lord of the Rings* books (Tolkien, 1954–1955) with his peers and played *The Lord of the Rings* board and video games with his friends. Jermaine described going to the library with friends to find books related to his favorite video games. For other students technological practices, some that involved literacy, may have replaced the sharing of books. For example, while Alicia spent every morning in 1st grade choosing books and reading them with her friends, she made fewer and fewer references to sharing books with friends as she moved through school. In middle school, she noted, "[My friends and I] don't read nothing." Reading books was not an act of affiliation. Simultaneously, Alicia described her favorite activities as chatting with her friends on the Internet, visiting websites, and singing and stepping with her friends—ironically, most of these activities involve literacy.

When asked what their friends read, the students generally identified magazines or maintained that their friends did not read anything. For some students there was an unacknowledged tension between their self-described affinity for books and their often adamant denial that their friends read books. Cultural models of reading and readers invoke identities and affiliations that accompany the reading of particular texts and particular literacy practices. Thus, while book reading was often a significant practice that students reported enacting at home, it was not something they shared with their peers or that their peers tended to share with them. Affiliations and identities enacted with peers, with two exceptions (Peter, Jermaine), did not involve reading books. However, despite this relative silence in regard to sharing books with peers, the tendency for students to identify popular series books as favorite texts, as described above, attests to the social nature of their reading preferences.

READING MAGAZINES AND OTHER TEXTS

Magazines were textual artifacts that were often particularly attractive to students (Davila & Patrick, 2010; Gabriel & Allington, 2009; Hall & Coles, 1999). They carry meanings that are partially derived from the fact that they are not books. Magazines carry meanings that are generally out-side the borders of school and often reference the present, current events, and popular culture. Worthy and her colleagues (Worthy, 1996; Worthy et al., 1999) argued that some of the appeal of magazines relates to the variety and specialization of magazines—including their ability to target the inter-ests of contemporary students. While most of the students in this sample re-ported reading magazines, there was little agreement on preferences. Alicia read *Nickelodeon Magazine.* Jermaine read *Time,* gaming magazines, and the real estate guides that his mother brought home from the grocery store. Marvin read comic books and advertisements that came in the newspaper or were posted on the Internet. Angela read *Young Miss* (*YM*) but admitted that she skimmed the articles reading only the sections that interested her. David eagerly awaited his *Sports Illustrated* magazine each month and read movie reviews from other magazines. He reported that he sometimes read cooking magazines, saying, "I cooked a whole meal from one of them." Peter reported that he and his friends shared magazines that focused on popular music. Four of the nine students, including the three students who struggled the most with reading, reported reading the newspaper; they fa-vored the sports and the local news sections.

Interest in texts extended beyond books and magazines in one poignant example; Christy, whose biological mother was then living in the Southeast-ern United States, described reading and rereading the greeting cards she has received from her mother and her mother's relatives. She showed me her collection of 16 cards that she and her sister had received. She read some of the notes in the cards into my tape recorder and explained that she still missed her mother despite having lived in a foster home and later an adop-tive home for the past 5 years.

In cases such as David reading cooking magazines and Jermaine read-ing the apartment rental guides, students read magazines that their moth-ers brought home. These reading preferences reflected the availability of particular texts and thus, the reading preferences of their parents. In the following section, I examine the relationships between student and parent reading preferences.

PARENTS' AND STUDENTS' SHARED READING PREFERENCES OVER TIME

Thus far, attention to time in this chapter has focused on changes in stu-dents' text reading practices and the types of texts they enjoy in middle school. However, time was also discernible in relation to the sources of students' reading interests. A short-term study conducted with these same students might suggest that the students did not share the reading interests of their parents. Patterns that were discernible with long-term data were not always evident in the short term. At the time of the middle school interviews, Christy was reading series books including *The Baby-sitter's Club* (Martin & Lerangris, 1986–2000) and *Junie B. Jones* (Park, 1992–current) books; her adopted mother read the Bible and women's magazines. Likewise, whereas Javon enjoyed *Harry Potter* books (Rowling, 1997–2007) and novels by Walter Dean Myers, his mother reportedly read only the paperwork she encountered at work. However, the longitudinal nature of this project revealed additional information. When I considered the reading practices reported by parents over time, patterns became apparent. While Christy's reading practices did not reflect the reading preferences of her adopted mother, her interests in *The Baby-sitter's Club* and *Junie B. Jones* books were comparable to those of her biological mother. Ms. Green had saved a stack of tattered novels from her own childhood featuring female protagonists for Christy (e.g., Judy Blume, Beverly Cleary). Despite not living with her mother since 3rd grade, it seemed that her mother's reading preferences continued to influence Christy. Likewise, while Ms. Mason reported that she had recently been "really involved" with her job and had no time to read, her reading interests reported at past interviews included suspense and mystery novels reflecting Javon and his brother's middle school enthusiasm for Harry Potter (Rowling, 1997–2007) and *Holes* (Sachar, 1998).

Alicia and her mother shared an interest in romance novels featuring African American characters. While Alicia's mother referred disparagingly to Alicia's books as "love novels," she enjoyed books by Jackie Collins and Terry McMillan—texts that some would place in the romance genre. Ms. Rodriguez's favorite author was Donald Goins. She shared his "city stories" with her friends, her sons, and eventually with Alicia. Peter, his mother, and grandmother enjoyed suspense and mystery novels. Marvin read *Goosebumps*, reflecting his grandfather's past fascination with the horror novels of Stephen King. When Jermaine excitedly told me about reading a book about Frederick Douglass, his father joined our conversation describing where Frederick Douglass' home had once stood in the local community. Furthermore, Jermaine's mother shared this interest in African American history; at a previous interview she had reported staying up all night to watch *Roots*. Only Bradford, one of the most challenged readers in the sample, did not seem to share a reading connection with his mother; however, he and his mother religiously watched the evening news and his mother regularly read the newspaper from "cover to cover."

David's and his mother's reading interests were less similar; although they both reported reading novels, David generally preferred science fiction while his mother noted that she was a big fan of Danielle Steele. She liked the books and the movies because they were about "rich people." As she noted, "I'm not rich—might as well watch them." Reading both science fiction and romances of rich people involve reading as an escape from daily life. David also read his mother's cooking magazines.

Perhaps the clearest example of shared reading preferences within families, was evident in Angela's family. Angela's mother reported that she was never an avid reader until she was married; her husband hooked her on science fiction and fantasy. Now she regularly reads fantasy novels as well as Angela's books that she finds lying around the house. As she explained, "I need something to read in the bathtub." Over the course of the interviews, she reported reading Angela's books from the *Harry Potter* Series (Rowling, 1997–2007) and *A Series of Unfortunate Events* books (Snicket, 1999–2006). Angela's younger sister had also read these books, and as we spoke, the girls and their mother recalled their favorite parts occasionally reciting lines from the texts.

Notably, the reading practices of parents changed significantly over time. While at an earlier phase of the project, Ms. Mason produced a book that she had finished the night before, a few years later she explained that she had not been reading much. While in the past Ms. Johnson reported being an avid reader, the demands of work and grandchildren became prohibitive when David was in middle school. Clearly reading practices change over time in relation to demands imposed by other dimensions of people's lives. This longitudinal tracking of reading practices complicates distinctions that are often made between people who are readers and those who are not. My data suggest that these categories are susceptible to situations and complications across the life course. While some researchers such as Strommen and Mates (2004) conclude that the differences between self-identified readers and nonreaders are due to differences in home reading practices (e.g., access to books, being read to as children), the current analysis complicates this indicating that home reading practices wax and wane over time in conjunction with other roles and responsibilities. More matters than the amount of time people spend reading. The reading practices that people adopt and adapt over long periods of time may be more important indicators of people's literate identities.

By conducting a longitudinal study, I was able to identify relationships between children's reading preferences and those of their parents that would have been invisible in the 8th-grade data. Over time, the reading interests of parents appeared to affect the reading preferences of children and these social relationships around reading sometimes extended to other family members and peers. Books circulated in Angela's and Alicia's homes. David and Jermaine read the magazines bought by their mothers. Peter described reading books from *The Lord of the Rings* (Tolkien, 1954–1955) and playing *The Lord of the Rings* Series with his friends. While, each child has developed his or her own affiliations towards books, these affiliations involved other people and relationships with family and friends.

CONCLUSION

Texts including series books, magazines, schoolbooks, and media-related books were primary artifacts in this study. Participants accessed cultural models related to reading, and used books and other texts to represent themselves as particular types of readers, students, and people. The students in this sample negotiated complex social and institutional contexts as they engaged with and rejected various texts. While each student was a unique reader with his or her own interest and disinterests, the students' preferences reflected their familial, social, and institutional worlds. As artifacts, books carried a range of meanings. Over time, schoolbooks, drawing on a cannon of classic and historically-oriented texts, increasingly referenced academic identities, and several students distanced themselves from these texts. Students complained about textbooks that were written for purely pedagogical purposes (e.g., textbooks, reading anthologies), viewing them as boring. While classic literature was often critiqued, a few students found these texts engaging, and most students appreciated at least a few of the texts they read in school. Series books in particular were contrasted to schoolbooks. Perhaps because they often fell outside the official school curriculum and were critiqued by adults, these books carried important social messages among peers and were markers of affiliation. Magazines also appealed to students. Few students in this sample had home access to the Internet. Finally, longitudinal analysis revealed intriguing connections between the reading preferences and practices of parents and those of their children. These positionings relative to texts referenced cultural models related to being a good reader and a good student, as well as discourses about being a teenager and fitting in with peers.

CHAPTER 4

Teaching and Time

Throughout the study, when asked about school, students spoke about their teachers. Their comments were sometimes humorous and entertaining. During the final middle school interview, I asked students what advice they would give their teachers; Jermaine responded, "I'll tell them [teachers] to keep their rooms clean. Yep and keep their calculators in order, their papers . . . like don't let it be spread all around the room and on the floor." Marvin offered warnings, "Don't sit no student next to someone they don't get along with . . . don't leave your desk drawer open with rubber bands [in it]. Don't let no student sit at your desk, the stuff might come [up] missing."

Other comments were more serious, sometimes holding teachers responsible for situations that were beyond their control; Javon said, "Teachers should buy new school supplies for their own class . . . because some of the material be old. And then some of the books, they be ripped and torn and when one of the pages is missing, they tell us to go work with someone else." Teachers are the primary school representatives that students encounter and students sometimes blame them for negative situations. Javon does not seem to have a full awareness of school budgets, the price of textbooks, and the minimal control that teachers generally have over materials and resources. His comments do not acknowledge the frustration that his teachers might also be experiencing.

The commitment teachers were expected to have to their students was identified by several participants; these students and parents drew upon the *discourse of the paycheck.*

> *Ms. Johnson*: But a lot of these teachers are just there for the paycheck.
> *Jermaine*: They [teachers] just want the money, they're not trying to teach you.
> *Ms. Rodriguez*: So we're saying that when we used to go to school, it's like the teacher was there to teach, not just get her paycheck. And it seem like they [teachers today] just get their paychecks.
> *Ms. Mason*: Because we've had people that really care, that you know that they want to see the kids. Then you have the one that's just there for the paycheck.

This recurring discourse of teachers and paychecks highlights the message that teachers should want to teach for reasons beyond money. By using the adverb *just,* participants denoted the intensity and degree to which teachers did not seem to be dedicated to their work. Limiting their efforts to "just there for the paycheck" or "just want the money" deny other reasons for teaching which participants describe as being "there to teach," being a teacher that "really care[s]," or "want[ing] to see the kids." Although some participants note that this critique applies to only some teachers, it was a repeated critique that was voiced similarly and referenced a cultural model of teaching that differentiates between callous, uncaring teachers and teachers who are committed to working with and teaching students.

MEMORIES OF FAVORITE TEACHERS

While critiques of teachers were often voiced, many students spoke fondly of certain past teachers. Some teachers assumed almost iconic statuses in the minds of their former students. One teacher, Mr. Lockman—a male African American, kindergarten teacher whose family was historically connected to the local African American community—was revered years later by some of his former students, all boys. When the children were in grade 1, parents spoke positively about Mr. Lockman:

> *Ms. Horner*: Peter could say his ABCs and that's one thing that
> Mr. Lockman said about him in kindergarten, like that
> Peter knew so much coming in already. I love that.
> *Ms. Johnson*: Mr. Lockman helped him [David] to know his
> ABCs last year very well. He was a very good teacher.

Even Mr. Sherwood, whose grandson Marvin had never been one of Mr. Lockman's students, reported to me when Marvin was in grades 1 and 5 that he had run into Mr. Lockman in the community. Students sometimes asked me about Mr. Lockman or they commented on their fond memories of him. David noted, "I remember he used to give us nuggins (laughs)" and later commented, "I loved him." Jermaine reported, "I know Mr. Lockman [was] real good." In the years since the kids had been in kindergarten, Mr. Lockman had retired. David wished that his younger brother, who was struggling in school, could have had Mr. Lockman as a teacher, "If he would have had him, *whoosh!*" As David's "whoosh" suggests, Mr. Lockman was not remembered for his kindness and patience, but for the discipline he established in the classroom and the high expectations he held for his kindergarten students.

Yet David's memories of Mr. Lockman were not entirely positive. When he was in 5th grade, David remarked, "When we was bad, he used to go like this to my head (pretends to hit himself)." Ms. Johnson agreed saying, "'cause you learned [in his class]" and "he'd give you that look. He was so stern." She later added, "But he was cool, I liked him." Several parents drew on cultural models related to gender arguing that a strict male presence was good for their sons. Ms. Hudson commented, "I think a man can do better for Jermaine than a female," while Ms. Johnson spoke about David's little brother saying, "I think he needs a man teacher."

David applauded his 4th-grade teacher, Ms. Gardener. By all accounts, Ms. Gardener was a remarkable teacher. Not only was she well-known for providing excellent professional development in-services to teachers across the district, but she had been selected as the State Teacher of the Year a couple of years after David was in her class. Ms. Gardener was known across the district for her hands-on, progressive approaches to teaching science, social studies, and literacy. Each year, she raised money and took her 4th-grade students on a trip. The year David was in her class, they visited a farm in Massachusetts. The trip lasted 3 days and involved a long bus ride. David spoke about Ms. Gardener and this trip at almost every subsequent interview. In addition to the trip, David noted that Ms. Gardener had some great stories and allowed her students to sing in class.

Peter spoke of a teacher he had when he was attending school in New York City. Ms. Donald was his English teacher and the first teacher to take an interest in Peter's writing. As he noted, "I especially like Ms. Donald. She let you be free to express your feelings and things like that. . . . Before I left she said I was her best student in class. She told me I could be a writer with all the stuff I would be coming up with." This comment was recalled during later interviews in high school when Peter announced his dream of becoming a journalist. For Peter, this was not a simple memory, it was a moment of reframing, when a teacher he admired and respected told him he *could* be a writer. Ms. Donald's words inspired meanings and identities in the present that suggested possibilities for the future.

As McLeod and Thomson (2009) lament, "the notion that the past and the future are always apprehended in the present has not always found its ways into empirical paradigms" (p. 8). In the current study, the lens is focused on precisely this dimension of students' and families' experiences. Past teachers are alive and interact with the present as students like David and Peter draw on the past as they discuss their current school experiences and teachers.

Teachers' pasts were also relevant to the ways students viewed their teachers. As reported in Chapter 1, when Javon recalled a favorite teacher, he focused on how Mr. Whitney had shared with Javon and his classmates the challenges he had faced and the fights he had been involved in while growing up. Javon believed that his testimonial contributed to the good relationships this teacher had with his students. Angela reported a similar experience with a math teacher who had shared personal information with the class. As Angela explained, the class was "really good with" this teacher, "You know, her sister got in a [car] accident. I always try to think of that." Angela's account was interesting in terms of the ways students and teachers were positioned. While we generally conceptualize teachers as working well with students, Angela turned the table. She granted agency to the students, stating that the students were "really good with" the teacher. It was the students who recognized the personal challenges faced by this teacher and accommodated her with appropriate sensitivity.

In both these accounts, students feel affinity with their teachers based on their teachers' willingness to disclose personal information over time (e.g., talking about their own pasts) and across spaces (e.g., sharing personal information from outside of school). To Javon and Angela, these teachers become people who have lives that extend beyond their roles as teachers and warrant relationships that draw on these human characteristics. Metcalfe and Game (2007) critiqued the ways time is allocated and managed in schools. They examined interviews with expert teachers, arguing that these teachers focused on ongoing classroom experiences rather than imposed goals and learning standards. Expert teachers used their time to build relationships with students and recognized the complexities and uncertainties that accompanied teaching. They worked to make the most of available time to help students learn rather than treating time as a commodity that could be directly translated into student learning.

PROVIDING, MAKING, TAKING, AND GIVING TIME

Perhaps the most prevalent and striking references to time and teaching relate to the ways students and parents describe teachers' proclivity to provide, make, take, and give time to students. In the following section, I use discourse analysis focused on temporal language (e.g., "go slow," "not hurry up," "help kids more," "every time") and implied temporal references (e.g., "you've got enough attention," "goes over [reviews] what we have done," "don't just brush them [kids] off") to examine four temporal dimensions of students' interactions with teachers.

- *Providing time* referred to allowing students time to work through difficult concepts. These data often focused on teachers who moved too quickly through material or failed to review material that had been taught.

- *Making time* referenced teachers carving out time to help students according to their individual needs. This was sometimes described as occurring despite large class sizes and curricular demands.

- *Taking time* to get to know students as individuals included calling parents when problems occurred at school.

- *Giving time* had two dimensions. It referred to teachers spending time with students outside of class and teacher's willingness to barter time with students. Several students appreciated teachers who would reward them for good work and effort by allowing them to use some class time for social activities.

Providing Time

Several students were concerned that their teachers did not provide them with the time they needed to learn material and complete tasks. Jermaine, a struggling student who was eventually retained multiple times in middle school, critiqued the temporal expectations that his teachers imposed. When asked what advice he would give his teachers, Jermaine said, "I'll tell them to slow down with the math, go slow for some students that don't get it, and help the students that don't get it." He complained that in language arts "we do like a book like for a week, [then] we go to another subject," and when he asked his Spanish teacher about a vocabulary word, he reported that she "say it all fast." As he reported, "they do like a week of this and then next week they do something that's different"; "they just go too fast." As Jermaine lamented, "They must think we [are] smart."

Jermaine's comment not only addressed the pace of instruction and the tendency for teachers to move forward despite the challenges faced by students, but also referenced a self-assessment based on his difficulty in keeping up. Jermaine attributed his inability to keep up to a deficit in his ability to learn material—not being "smart."

Other students echoed Jermaine's comments. David, a more successful student, made the following comment about teachers and the pace of instruction. "[Teachers] have to be ready. [They] have to have good plans to make people learn. Not hurry up and just get going—do nows, do stuff." Confused, I was not sure what David meant by "Do nows." I asked him to clarify, and David explained, "Do nows? Like when you come to class, you have to do this *right now*!"

Ms. Holt reported that Bradford had shared similar concerns with her about his teachers. As she reported, he had complained, "They don't even teach how to [do it] or explain it to you. He's [the teacher] making me go too fast." Ms. Holt lamented that, "When they do it too fast, he don't understand it. He gets disgusted, and it's all over with. It's a [w]rap." While Jermaine assumed that he was not smart enough to learn the material his teacher presented, Bradford became frustrated and virtually gave up trying to learn. Ms. Holt's phrase, "it's a [w]rap" simultaneously referenced multiple discourses—a photographer ending a photo shoot by stating "it's a wrap," meaning that the photo shoot had been successfully completed and "it's a rap," indicating both the conclusion of the interaction and the ironies that are named and evoked in rap music. This second meaning references the end of the conversation, a decision having been made, and a lack of recourse for further action resulting in Bradford becoming "disgusted" with schooling and teachers.

The multiple meanings and the immediacy invoked by the word [w]rap reflect David's do nows and Jermaine's report that teachers "must think we [are] smart" because they move so quickly through material. As Jermaine reported, providing time makes a difference; he reports that his favorite teacher tells "me to take my time." Providing time entails not only allowing students time to work through difficult concepts, but as the recounted words of Jermaine's teacher ("take *my* time") indicate, it is Jermaine's time. In Jermaine's linguistic construction, time does not belong to the teacher or the school; time belongs to the student and should be available for students to use.

Making Time

Making time requires teachers to designate time to help students, explain concepts, and meet the needs of individual students. Teachers must actively carve out time to ensure that not only is material presented but that students are helped to master that material. Parents intrinsically retained faith in students' ability to learn, and worried that their children's abilities were not recognized or developed. Throughout the comments presented below, parents recognize structural issues including large class sizes, curricular demands, and large student/teacher ratios. While they attested to teaching as hard work, they did not relieve teachers of their responsibilities and were adamant that teachers must find ways to help children learn.

Mr. Sherwood, whose mother was a teacher, was particularly sensitive to the challenges teachers faced. "It's hard being a teacher because like I says I know I could never be a teacher. That would be out of my mind." He explained that he would love Marvin to be in a class with two teachers saying, "that would be great for him." Similarly, Jermaine explained that having a second teacher in his classes would be helpful. Jermaine's mother, Ms.

Hudson, highlighted the importance of individualized instruction—working with children one-on-one as needed. The mother of a student who had consistently struggled in school, she reported that "a good teacher, she can't go to everybody at the same time, Okay? She has to do individual, you know."

While both students and parents recognized the challenges created by large classes and understaffing, they held teachers responsible for teaching. As David reported, "To me teachers do what they got to do. I understand that they don't feel like teaching it thousand times because they get tired of it, but they should [teach], that's what they get paid for." Jermaine, perhaps due to his frustrations with school, was less understanding. His advice to teachers was to "help them [students] out." He continued, "Like if you ask for [help on] the problem, they like say, 'Do this and divide this.' They don't like show you or nothing—just tell you. They need to show you . . . [and] do not tell us, a child, to shut up." Jermaine presented his interactions with teachers as spiraling downward:

> I'm trying to talk through it but sometimes he's [the teacher's] like, "What? What you want? You've got enough attention." I be like, "I'm just going to ask you something." "So what? Don't argue with me. Do not argue with me." "I'm not." "You are arguing with me. [Do] you want to be kicked out of class?" "No, I don't." "Then shut up." So I just shut my mouth.

Jermaine suspected that his teachers "just don't like helping me." He was not the only participant who expressed these types of concerns.

> *Christy*: [Teachers have to] break it down to us.
> *Ms. Johnson*: [I've heard teachers say] "If you don't get it while I am teaching, oh well."
> *Bradford*: They should help us more to read and help us sound out the words more better.

Marvin noted that teachers generally paid attention to him only when he was doing something bad.

Conversely, David draws on this discourse to describe his favorite teacher, "He tries to give us help on what we need help on, questions, and he goes over what we have done before we take a test and stuff." This account positions the teacher as a partner in helping students master material in order to do well on tests. Not only does the teacher present information, but he ensures that students understand that material. As David noted, "Very few [teachers] explain what's on the test."

While David did well in school and generally appreciated his teachers, he worried about peers who struggled in school. He described kids who "just don't want to do it [the work]." He reported "so many teachers don't even want to help them, they [the teachers] know they [the students are] smart but they still be failing them. I don't know what their problem is." His mother, who was sitting nearby, chimed in, "A lot of the problem is these teachers don't care." David suggested that teachers should "try to get kids into programs if they know they [kids] got problems." Alicia noted that teachers should "try to help the [kids] more with their work "'cause some kids if they help them enough, some kids won't fail."

Making time for students requires teachers to help students when they encounter difficulties, explain concepts, and work with individual students. In this role, teachers are positioned as resources that students can draw upon to learn material and prepare for tests. They are trying to help children succeed not merely document what students have failed to learn. This involves taking time with students, explaining things, and breaking "it down to us."

Taking Time

Taking time involved getting to know students as individuals. It entailed talking with students, learning about their lives, and being in contact with their families. Christy's adopted mother, Ms. Denver, described taking time:

> [A] good teacher [is] one who shows interest in the kid and when they come tell them and ask them a question, they don't just brush them off. They stand and listen to the kid's problems and stuff. If you know there's something they can't handle, you know, maybe [they] call the parent and get in touch with the parent.

Alicia noted that teachers should "talk to the kids one-on-one." Marvin agrees saying, "You should already listen to a student before they go and do something [they shouldn't]."

Peter, a successful student, drew on multiple timescales comparing his teachers with images of teachers from the past. His use of the term "nowadays" highlights this comparison:

> Nowadays, they're [teachers are] like talking like the students and things. And they know mostly what's going on in the schools [and in] a lot of students' lives and I don't think they could do anything more. I mean they're acting like a student now.

While Peter believed that impersonal teachers who did not relate to students were occasionally problems, he explained, "most of the time they are our friends." Peter shared suggestions for how teachers could learn about their students' lives, "Visit where they live, talk to the people they talk to, know what they [are] going through. Know about their life and their struggles, things like that."

This positioning of teachers as "acting like students" and as "friends" raises interesting questions. As friends, teachers support students and help students to be successful. Although some educators might argue that if teachers fulfill friendship roles, their authority as teachers could be compromised, some of the parents in this sample seemed to disagree. Several parents agreed with Peter. Ms. Sherwood, Marvin's grandmother, noted, "You got to be a teacher, a tutor, a friend, somebody that care about you. "'Cause teachers should tell that kid [why they are coming to school] and that way they'll learn, because that's where their focus [is]." Ms. Hudson noted that the relationships Jermaine has with his teachers are critical, "there's teachers he [Jermaine] has good relationships [with]; there's some that he has bad relationships [with]. I think those are the classes he be real stubborn in."

Ms. Holt, Bradford's mother, worried specifically about teachers who taught in low-income communities. She noted: "They need patience because there's some of these kids, they come from hard, hard, hard lives. And these teachers aren't educated to deal with the hard life this kid is going through . . . they don't understand the children of this city." She noted that the teachers are in the community from 7:30 until 3:30 but that she has "never seen a teacher walk to the corner store . . . which they should do . . . this way you kind of know what these kids that you're dealing with *are* going through everyday."

Marvin, who in grade 8 was struggling with both school and with the law, did not have strong relationships with his teachers. As he indicated, "Like if I'm not in the mood to read, I won't read. I won't even look at the book. I turn around, turn the page or something." He continued, "I don't pay no attention to my teachers. I don't like looking at my teachers." Concerned, I asked "Why not?" This question was followed by silence. I tried again, "What do you think they're about? Are they trying to help you? Or don't they really like you? Or what do you think is going on?" Marvin mumbled, "I don't know." Not even wanting to look at his teachers belies a serious lack of relationships between Marvin and his teachers.

Another way that teachers took time, was by staying in contact with families. Throughout the interviews, parents spoke about the importance of teachers calling home. Ms. Hudson described "nice" teachers as being willing to call, "Some of them [teachers] have been nice. Only when he [Jermaine] get out of hand, he talks back and don't do what they tell him to do, then they have to call me. I'd say maybe once a month." Ms. Rodriguez reported that she knew that Alicia had good teachers if they called her when there was a problem. Before 8th grade even started, one of Alicia's teachers called home. Ms. Rodriguez thought this was great, "She [the teacher] was like, 'If you have any problems take down my number' she says, 'I'm not going to only call you for a bad report. I'm going to call you for good report,' and I'm like, 'okay.'"

Between the 5th-grade interviews and the 8th-grade interviews, Angela's family moved from the city into a suburban community. Ms. Burns identified the propensity for teachers to call home as a difference between urban and suburban teachers, "They [suburban teacher] seemed willing to pick up the phone and call, whereas last year, they're like, 'We can't do that. I have 150 students. I can't call every student's parent.'"

Taking time with students involves getting to know students as individuals and forming personal and friendly relationships with both students and their parents. It means learning about their lives including understanding "the children of this city." Parents in this sample spoke adamantly about the importance of calling parents.

Giving Time

As described above, giving time has two dimensions. Not only does it refer to teachers spending time with students outside of school, but it also captures teachers' willingness to barter time with students. Some teachers would barter time with students—rewarding students for good work and effort by allocating class time to activities that the students enjoyed.

Some students recalled teachers who would spend time with them outside of school. Bradford described a special education teacher that he had worked with for the past 2 years, "She used to take me ice skating and speed skating." Bradford's mother recognized and appreciated this attention, "She was a caring teacher. Kept on that boy. She was around at least once a week so that let me know she was very concerned too." Likewise it was during the 8th-grade interviews when Christy spoke of the time she had spent with me outside of school. Her mother had been going through a difficult time as she struggled with the death of her boyfriend, being bipolar, and being evicted from her apartment. During this time, Christy sometimes spent time with my family and me. She remembered visiting the library and spending the night at my house. Notably, Christy often used me as resource for learning about her past. She routinely asked me questions about her former teachers, being retained in 1st grade, and about her mother. By then, I was the only person she regularly spoke with who had known her when she and her sister lived with their mother.

Several parents recalled teachers who spent time with them when they were in school. Ms. Hudson, Jermaine's mother, recalled a teacher who invited her over to spend nights in her home when she was in elementary school. She noted that her daughter had a teacher like that as well. David's mother, Ms. Johnson, had a kindergarten teacher who would sit and read books with her after school.

In addition to recognizing teachers who spent time with them outside of school, many students valued teachers who bartered time—making deals with students so that if they worked hard and completed assignments or units of study, they would be rewarded with using class time in enjoyable ways. In other words, using class time wisely was rewarded by dedicating time to activities that the students enjoyed.

> *Javon*: Like every time that the teachers give us something to do and when we finish it, they should give us like a 2-minute break.
>
> *Jermaine*: [When we are good] we drink pop, [eat] cookies, watch TV, do work, activities, a lot of stuff . . . [and] go on field trips.
>
> *Javon*: Sometimes he [the teacher] gives us candy, but if we really good, he lets us sit around and talk for a couple minutes.
>
> *Christy*: At the end of class [my English teacher] she has a fun prize. And if we get our prize, next we get 5 minutes—we get to leave class 5 minutes early.
>
> *Jermaine*: She was a nice teacher. She let us have parties and stuff.
>
> *David*: Most times they will give us a break, let us watch a movie on a book we already read.
>
> *Javon*: The best part is when it's lunchtime. They let the kids go outside if they're done with lunch, we just sit around and socialize until lunch is over.

Peter highlighted this negotiation between teachers and students. He argued that bartering time could help teachers manage student behavior. As he reported, "[Teachers should] sometimes give us a break. The students won't take advantage of them, but every once in a while, yeah, you have your class clown and they'll probably do something." While Peter does not suggest that bartering will solve all behavior problems, he argued that it would address problems with most of the children.

Marvin described bartering occurring in the chill-out room. Students were sent to the chill-out room when they had misbehaved in class—sometimes for 2 or 3 days of class time. "When you finish [your work], he has his own TV so you don't have to bring in no TV from the AV room. If we did good that Thursday, it would be [TV] all day Friday [or] some [time] in the morning and some in the afternoon."

Finally, while teachers can give time, they can also take it away. Several students complained that teachers assigned "too much homework," infringing on their free time outside of school. Jermaine was particularly annoyed at a teacher who assigned too much work over a holiday weekend, "I don't like her 'cause she give us too much homework and junk. Last Friday she like give us like two packages of homework about a book that we read and do an essay and do a book report. How was I going to finish all that and it's due on Tuesday. I did do the packet and did the essay."

In these accounts, time is treated as a commodity that teachers could either give or take. They could spend time with students outside of the school day, barter time in school, or consume students' time outside of school. Teachers are described as using time to build relationships with students, forge bargains, and infringe on students' lives outside of school.

ASSUMING AUTHORITY AND DOING THEIR JOBS

As illustrated above, students described the kinds of relationships they desired with teachers and the help and support they expected. Jermaine expected his teachers to keep their classrooms tidy and show the students how to do the work. Several participants voiced a discourse related to paychecks arguing that teachers should be more concerned about their students. David explained that teachers should "explain what's on the test" and teach. Other parents mentioned teachers calling parents and taking an interest in students.

However, an additional discourse also operated, sometimes in tension with discourses that focused on creating caring relationships and supporting students. This discourse involved teachers assuming authority. For example, drawing on discourses of urban students, Alicia complained that teachers "act like they don't like the kids or they're scared of them." She explained, "when the kids fight in class, they don't try to break them up. They don't. They think that the kids will try to hurt them or something." Her younger sister described a similar situation in her elementary school classroom, "Instead of the teachers yell[ing] at the kids, the kids yell at the teachers."

Christy described some of her teachers as having a "hard time teaching the students because they will start acting up. And not listen to you 'cause you got to be more strict." Christy described her classmates gathering around the classroom door before the bell rang and the teacher physically blocking the doorway, "She [the teacher] tries to stop them. She stands in front of the door." Several students expressed these types of concerns.

Javon: Some of the teachers are good but some of them will
     just let the kids do anything. They [teachers] should make

sure they have their teacher's schedules ready for their
kids for the next day. 'Cause some of the teachers, they do
their own teacher's schedules [lesson planning] in class.
David: She [his teacher] is so good [but] she need to take control
of her class. She can't let them kids run her over . . . send
them to the office or give them detention or something.
Jermaine: Tell the kid if they don't want to learn [to]
get out [of] the classroom. (Pause) That's it.
Christy: Give the student only two chances and [if] they
blow those two chances, put them out [of] the class.

Discourses related to teacher authority involve drawing a fine line and
some teachers were described as being unreasonably strict. Marvin described
a teacher who would not let him use the restroom. Alicia described a teacher
who made the students raise their hands for permission to get a tissue or
throw something in the trash. Javon reported that sometimes teachers are
too hard on students and they should be careful about "embarrassing them
in front of their friends and stuff." Peter described a teacher who "never
smiles and like he's always watching." Peter said that in this class he'd "just
turn around and do my work."

Students expected their teachers to do their jobs. Alicia directly addressed teachers' responsibilities and suggested that they should change the
ways they act—"[teachers should] help the kids more and do their job." She
approved of her school principal, saying that the principal "do[es] what she
[is] supposed to do. She take care of the school [and] do her job. I don't hear
her say nothing bad about kids and they don't say nothing bad about her."
David noted that one of his teachers would tell the class, whether you learn
or not, "'I'm going to teach and whoever listens they gonna get it.'" David
viewed this as unacceptable. As he argued, "You're supposed to make sure
everyone listens." David praised teachers who "give a lot of work." As he
explained, assigning work assured that students have "more things to do"
which he described as a good thing.

Finally, comments about teacher authority occur alongside discourses
about fairness. Teacher fairness has been identified as a significant issue by
researchers (Dalbert, 2004; Elkind, 1971; Feldlaufer, Midgley, & Eccles,
1988). For example, Feldlaufer and her colleagues (1988) found that after
the transition to middle school children reported that teachers "care less
about them, are less friendly, and grade them less friendly than the teachers
they have had the last year of elementary school" (pp. 149–150). As Javon
explained, "If one kid makes trouble, they [should] let the one kid get in
trouble by themselves. They don't [shouldn't] punish the whole class for
what that one kid did." Likewise, fairness is negotiated between students

and their teachers. As Alicia noted, "They [teachers] should be respectful if they want kids to be respectful of them" and "let the kids be who they are instead of trying to change them."

SCHOOL AS BORING

While authority was a predominant theme, several students commented on the types of the activities that occurred in class. Some of these discourses related to teachers who bored students and wasted their time. Angela advised teachers not to "drone when you are talking. [It's] annoying when they keep talking and talking and talking." She advocated "more hands-on activities." Christy complained that her Spanish class was "too long to sit there." Alicia described falling asleep in class when her teacher was boring.

Students identified a lack of activity as contributing to boring instruction. David complained about being assigned to read chapters in his science book and then answering questions in class. He was disappointed, "We don't do a lot of experiments. Only about two or three—no, about two." Angela wished that her teachers would require them to copy "less notes" off the board, "[They] have notes on the overhead. They'll say, 'Okay, you write this.' He just stayed writing it [and saying it] out loud." Marvin's grandmother raised a different issue. She was worried that Marvin was not being challenged in school. She complained that although he was in grade 8, his teacher gave him 5th-grade work. Marvin agreed, "Yeah, they do give me 5th-grade work in math problems . . . [I know] because I been reading her [the teacher's books]. There was this book on the front desk. It had 5th-grade work [in it]." In these examples, students identify artifacts of schooling—such as those involved in doing experiments—as fun versus copying off the board, math problems, and textbooks that relate to boring instruction.

In contrast, favorite teachers were almost universally described as funny or as making learning fun; discourses of fun, games, and play were used to describe their classrooms. For example, in 5th grade Marvin liked his homeroom teacher because she was funny and his writing teacher because they played games in class. Tiffany recalled a favorite teacher who "used to make us laugh." An emphasis on fun and games was also evident in the memories parents had of favorite teachers. Ms. Webster described her favorite teacher as making "things fun." "Every time she would get ready to teach us something she would put a game to it, and that's how we learned through games and stuff. It was a lot of fun and you learn fast that way." Similarly, Ms. Johnson described her 4th-grade teacher, Mr. Chase, who would "play word games and stuff with you. And it made it easier to learn. You wanted to learn."

CONCLUSION

In this chapter, I focused on the ways students and their families viewed teachers as operating in time. In general, students hold teachers accountable for what happens in school. Much of this is contingent on how time is used and delegated. Providing time, making time, taking time, and giving time are all presented as being within the purview of the teacher. Teachers can provide students with the time they need to learn, make time to help students, take time to know students and their families, and give time to students outside of school or in exchange for cooperation during school. Students and parents reference discourses related to working for more than a paycheck, boring classes, and fun, games, and play. Cultural models that evoke assumptions about gender and teaching, assuming authority in classrooms, and urban students who should be feared and controlled are also referenced. In some cases, students do not seem to recognize that teachers meeting students' expectations is contingent on support from school district administration. Oversized classes make meeting the needs of all students difficult. Likewise, a lack of school resources makes replacing old books or referring students for extra help impossible. While students are correct in critiquing their situations, in some cases, teachers are neither solely or ultimately responsible.

CHAPTER 5

Parents' Voices:
Memories and Making Sense

Among the most vivid memories of learning to read for the parents in this sample were memories of a particular artifact—*Dick and Jane* readers. Apparently the parents in this study are not unusual. The books were reissued in 2003 for the sake of nostalgia and with warnings from the publisher that they were not intended for reading instruction. A *USA Today* article (Toppo, 2004) notes that *Fun with Dick and Jane* and other books in the series are often remembered fondly by adults who used the book in school. However, this is not universally true; Toppo (2004) also quotes David Bloome as saying that "many people grew to dislike them and resent them" and that "many people struggled with those books. Many people found them boring. Many people found them not to speak to their experiences" (para. 6 & 7). Luke (1987) refers to the books as referencing a "particular official fiction—the whitewashed world of *Dick and Jane*, of untroubled Progressive childhood, of simplified nuclear family" (p. 91).

While not all of the parents in the current study were old enough to have read these books, the parents who were in their late 20s or older generally spoke about *Dick and Jane* when asked about learning to read. Many reported fond memories of the books.

> *Ms. Webster*: I remember having like "Spot," "can," "run." "See Spot run." Duh, duh, duh, you know, that book. Yeah, I enjoyed it. I mean it was easy. It was real thick and that was our reading book. And each day we would go in there and we would read a chapter . . .we went straight to the word. The teacher would go and say, "Okay, now we are going to sound it out," and then she would sound it out with us. That's how we learned to read.
>
> *Ms. Holt*: Whatever it was, it worked. Because I still remember the dog, Spot, and Dick and Jane and mom and dad and Sally, the baby. . . . It was good 'cause they always did something different and the words were kinda simple . . .

you know a little short story but they were always in them.
Jane never did anything much, but Dick always did.

Mr. Sherwood: It [the book series] was fun 'cause they were always
having fun in the story. He was always getting into trouble or with
something happening here, or Jane doing this, you know? Dick
went over to the store. All that, you know? It was fun, oh yeah.

In these accounts, fun and enjoyment are highlighted. The books are
described as easy and effective. The children in the stories were having fun
as were the readers. While this nostalgia was typical of most accounts, some
parents were simultaneously critical. Mr. Sherwood who above described
the books as fun later described reading the *Dick and Jane* books as contributing to one of his hardest years at school.

I got through that *Dick and Jane* book. That year was one of the hardest
years because they really wouldn't teach me anything. They just gave
you the book.

Ms. Johnson recalled the workbooks that accompanied the series, "I
just remember those thick workbooks . . . they seemed like they were never
ending." Ms. Hudson knew that she had read the *Dick and Jane and Sally*
[books] but could not remember anything about them.

None of the parents noted the critiques raised by Luke (1987) referencing the cultural models of family or citizenship that are so clearly presented
in the texts. They did not reflect on the propensity of characters in the book
to comply with authority and meet established norms of behavior. Parents
did not critique the empty, repetitive stories in which events of substance did
not occur. No one mentioned the representation of a narrow range of demographics related to race, class, and implied Christian religion. Knowing that
African American characters did not appear in the books until 1965 when
the series was already in decline, I asked some of the parents how they felt
about the lack of African American characters:

Mr. Sherwood: No, oh no, oh no, uh-uh. My mom always said when
we were in school, [whether] we White, Black, wealthy or any
[of] that, you were there for only one purpose—to learn. And
I say that [too] . . . yeah that's it. And you know, I always say,
"No, because you're going to deal with that all your life."
Ms. Holt: You know what? It never [occurred to me]. See
back when I was raised up, I wasn't raised up around
no Blacks. My mother she kept us you know kind of
distant (Ms. Holt's voice trails to a whisper).

Both Mr. Sherwood and Ms. Holt described the practices and teachings of their parents as mediating their exposure to books that did not represent them. While Mr. Sherwood's mother highlighted the ultimate goal of attending school—"to learn," Ms. Holt describes her mother as keeping her "distant" and perhaps insulated from and denying the significance of racially-based concerns. In both cases, parents provided their children with discourses of resilience that were relevant to both the materials they encountered in school and their future lives. Specifically, the lack of African American representation was not allowed to be an obstacle to learning to read.

Although memories are often recognized as being partial and inaccurate, some parents were remarkably accurate in their recollections of the *Dick and Jane* books. While people often assume that the *Dick and Jane* books presented a phonic approach to the teaching of reading, this was not true. The books actually relied on the gradual exposure to a controlled vocabulary to teach beginning readers. Ms. Mason provided a perceptive description of the "look/say" method used in these texts.

> I like it [the *Dick and Jane* book]. 'Cause it had some easy words, and it used them so many times that you had no choice but to learn . . . when they bring new words in . . . they had it so many times that by the time you're through with that book, you learned that word.

In addition to encountering the books in school, Ms. Holt remembers her mother teaching her to read with *"Dick and Jane* books at home." She also reported owning other artifacts related to the teaching of reading—her mother had purchased a full set of SRA cards for her children to use at home.

> Now it's Hooked on Phonics but [back then] there were yellow, blue, green, purple [cards]. The purple were the advanced, but you started with the red and the blue . . . my mother bought a set of those [cards] . . . [they were] very expensive but it was for all of us.

Memories of the *Dick and Jane* books reveal a great deal about the complexity of memory. Memories are not distinct, accurate, and easily reported representations of experiences. They are intertwined with things that have happened since, the ways we have made sense of our past over time, the types of people we view ourselves to be, and the futures we hope to achieve. Reports about *Dick and Jane* are incomplete (e.g., "It never [occurred to me]") and mired with contradictions (e.g., "It was fun"/"[It] was one of the hardest years").

As illustrated above, parents carry with them their memories of their own school experiences, and these experiences impact the ways they make sense of their children's school and literacy experiences. While there are many ways in which parents draw upon the past, I explore discourses of now and then, race and schooling, and how stories about teachers from the parents' pasts relate to the school experiences of their children. I end the chapter with comments from parents about teachers who seem to be getting younger and younger each year.

DISCOURSES OF *NOW AND THEN*

In the transcript presented above Ms. Holt reported, "Now it's Hooked on Phonics but [back then] there were yellow, blue, green, purple [cards]." Discourses, contrasting *now* with *then*, recur throughout the interviews. Smitherman (2006) identifies this as a common linguistic construction in African American speech. Specifically, she references the tendency for African America speakers to use the phrase "back in the day" to refer nostalgically to past times. In the interviews with my former students and their families, participants often contrasted now with then.

Now and then constructions were often used to contrast contemporary and past approaches to reading instruction.

> *Ms. Webster*: I mean it's different from what the kids
>   do today. I mean how we learned to read and how
>   they learn how to read are totally different.
> *Ms. Holt*: I guess they don't have the programs [now] as they had
>   back [then]. We're talking 30, 40 years ago—something like that.

Ambivalence is apparent in both quotes. Both argue that reading instruction is different for contemporary children, but neither parent identifies the difference as an improvement.

Ms. Holt described contemporary approaches to teaching reading as complicated. She referenced new approaches to teaching phonics and phonemic awareness—highlighting the *bib* and the *bob*—a method using decodable texts to teach children to rhyme and read.

> [It's] very difficult now. Because the way that they let the, like we were taught Tom, Dick, and Jane and that was simple. You know it was real simple. But now they got the *bib* and the *bob* and the instead of teaching them to read they teaching them to rhyme . . . like in kindergarten they like [should be] giving him the basics first before they making him

rhyme any. I'm not saying anyone can, but most kids if you teach them something over and over each day they'll remember it.

In the end, Ms. Holt advocates for repeated practice—echoing the look/say methods used in the *Dick and Jane* books. Reading programs and materials are artifacts that parents described as having the potential to help kids learn to read and being a successful teacher was related to using the right program.

Ms. Rodriguez uses a now/then discourse to highlight the technological advances and opportunities for students to access multimedia:

> If they were to have had something that I was interested in then, I probably would have stuck to it more. . . . I like computers, but back then they didn't have computers. No, and now [I] see the things that he's [points to one of her sons who is in high school] doing. They go to studios and make videos and stuff like that. They didn't have that when I was going to school. I would have loved that.

New artifacts of schooling that included computers, video equipment, and studios that students could use to create stuff were praised as potential tools for engaging students.

As presented in Chapter 4, now and then discourses were evident when participants compared contemporary teachers with teachers of the past. In those examples, past teachers were described as caring about students while contemporary teachers taught only for the money.

> I have heard a lot of these teachers say, when I've been in these schools, if you don't get it while I'm teaching the class oh well? . . . You know it's not like that. When I went to school you'd stay after school, you had some teachers that would come to your home. They don't do that anymore.

When comparing teachers of the past to teachers in the present, parents and students generally find today's teachers lacking.

Peter uses a now and then comparison to present his mother's opinion about his school. Peter loved his school, but his mother, who had grown up in the city in which the research was conducted, was less happy with her son's school. Peter, however, did not like the fighting that sometimes occurred at school. He compared the amount of fighting in his school now to the number of fights that occurred when his mother was in high school, "The worst part about [school's name]? The fights. Yeah. But it's not as much fights as there was last year. Or as much fights as my mom probably remembers it." He suspects that his mother's concerns with extensive fighting were due to the ways things were at his school many years ago. Unlike the examples presented comparing teachers, Peter suggests that the present situation at his school is better than what his mother remembers. Unlike Smitherman's (2006) discussion of back in the day, the comparisons of now and then documented in the current study can suggest that current times are better.

Now and then comparisons are also used to make grand statements about the current state of the world. Mr. Sherwood adopts a discourse about society and change to explain the difficulties faced by his grandson, Marvin.

> [Marvin needs to] find out for himself. For real, I understand you know, 'cause the way the world is now and the time it is now, you know what I mean? . . . You know and the ways kids is doing [things] today. You can't do it. Well, I know you, Ms. Lilly. You see the kids. You know it's a different world.

Mr. Sherwood enlisted my agreement by using the phrase "you know" and appealed to my knowledge of kids to highlight the challenges that students face in a world that has changed bringing whole new sets of challenges—he invoked a discourse of a fast-moving, complicated, and relentless modern world. At the time of this interview, Marvin had recently been arrested, and Mr. Sherwood was grappling with the effects of that situation and struggling to maintain faith in Marvin's essentially good qualities. Mr. Sherwood believed that part of the struggle Marvin faced was the increased pace at which things happen. As Mr. Sherwood reported, "Everything is just so fast. Every thing is happening now."

Like Mr. Sherwood, Ms. Mason used a now and then discourse to understand the challenges that her children faced. Rather than focusing on the differences between now and then, Ms. Mason placed herself back in time referencing a cultural model of adolescence, "When I was younger [I sometimes got in trouble]." She explained that she remembered what it was like being young, saying "I put myself in my kid."

Participants in this study used now and then discourses in various ways. Some parents use the discourse to contrast the ways they learned to read with the experiences of their children. Their words are marked by ambivalence. They describe today's programs as "different" but not always better. Some parents and students see positive dimensions of the new ways of doing things citing the possibility of using video and computers or describing schools that have improved. Other parents lamented the loss of simple ways of learning to read, a slower paced world, and fabled teachers who cared about their students.

RACE AND SCHOOLING

While parents did not identify the race of characters in the *Dick and Jane* series as problematic, race played a significant role in the educational experiences of some parents and in the ways they understood schooling for their children and grandchildren. Mr. Hudson, Jermaine's father, had grown up in the South and had attended school in the 1940s and 1950s. He shared with me the advice he gives Jermaine. "We keep telling him school's important. Get an education. You know what I mean? When I was growing up, I had an excuse. Weren't no money, you know. There wasn't." As he explained, "the White people went to school but the Black people had to work White people's farms while the White kids go to school."

Similarly, Ms. Sherwood, Marvin's grandmother attended a segregated school in the South. When I asked her what it was like to attend segregated schools, she responded:

> They was okay. We didn't know nothing [about] being together with nobody else anyway. So it was all right for us. We had good times and then [some] things were bad. It wasn't really different you know. Everything was okay but most of what I remember we worked home . . . .You would work home and keep the kids, and take care of the house and cook.

Unlike her White counterparts, Ms. Sherwood was required to work in the cotton fields with her brothers and parents. She worried about the education that Marvin was getting in his special education class and connected his experiences to race, "I've been reading up on it, and they mostly put Black kids in them kind of [special education] classes and then they sunk them and that's how you all [motioning toward Marvin] get behind." As Ms. Sherwood lamented, the time Marvin spent in special education classes with his African American peers resulted in his falling behind. As she reported, "It's bad on Black kids. It's really bad."

In both these accounts, a historical timescale is referenced to connect parents' racialized experiences of schooling to the educational experiences of their children. Mr. Hudson emphasized that school was important and that Jermaine needed to take advantage of the opportunity he had to get an education. Ms. Sherwood agreed that Marvin had opportunities that she did not, but complicated the discussion by raising questions about how African American children were treated in school. They may have access but that access was limited by their placement in special education.

WHAT MAKES A GOOD TEACHER?

When the children were in 1st grade, I asked their parents to tell me about memorable teachers from their past. In this section, I explore how the stories they told during our first interviews related to accounts shared over the 8-year study—informing the ways parents understand the school experiences of their children, and evaluate their children's teachers. Specifically, I document discoursal patterns related to being a good teacher that are prominent in particular families. Ms. Horner describes teachers who cared and assumed a maternal role with students. Ms. Johnson repeatedly draws on discourses that highlight teachers who went the "extra mile." Mr. Sherwood encourages teachers and administrators to "get involved." Ms. Rodriguez suggests that the materials teacher use to teach reading matter. Ms. Mason argues that learning depends on the teacher and how he or she presents and shares information. Finally, Ms. Holt describes a thin line between being a teacher who has confidence in children's abilities and teachers who are inflexibly hard on students.

Ms. Horner: "She was my mom at school"

> My 2nd-grade teacher, she was wonderful, and I have no idea what her name is. This is right before we moved out into [a suburban community] . . . she was my mom at school. I knew that she just looked out after me. Made me feel real special . . . she was a wonderful person.

Like many descriptions of wonderful teachers, Ms. Horner makes no reference to materials, instructional methods, or academic content. Accounts of exceptional teachers generally involve discourses related to relationships between students and their teachers.

The strong relationship that Ms. Horner shared with her 2nd-grade teacher was echoed in the way she described Peter's relationship with his teacher in grade 4, "She was great. Every time I talked with her, she always had nothing but good things to say about Peter." She reported that teachers need patience and understanding, and they must "be able to catch the child's attention so that the child will want to learn." Later that year Ms. Horner reported, "He's a Model Citizen every year. He's just—He's truly wonderful. He tutors [other kids] in school." Throughout school, Peter enjoyed positive relationships with his teachers.

Ms. Johnson: "Go the extra mile"

> Mr. Chase, 4th grade . . . he really went out of his way to help kids. He would come to your house, you know? And just in school, he would

make learning fun where [as] a lot of teachers didn't do that. You know he'd play word games and stuff with you. And it made it easier to learn. You wanted to learn. You know, he would always come by the house or whatever. It was real nice.

Like Ms. Horner's reports above, relationships matter. In particular, Ms. Johnson emphasized the extra things that Mr. Chase did that extended beyond his paycheck. He visited homes and made learning fun by incorporating games. As Ms. Johnson reminds us, a lot of teachers do not do these things, and these things do matter. Ms. Johnson also described her kindergarten teacher, "We used to sit there and we'd pick out books, and she'd sit there and we'd read together. I'd stay after school and do that with her. I loved it. She was my most favorite teacher throughout school."

These thoughts about teachers going beyond what is required are apparent in her comments about the willingness of teachers to call parents when there was a problem in school. As she asked, "What would it take? A 5-minute phone call?" Reflecting on her experiences with David's older siblings, she reported the "high school is the worst one . . . a lot of teachers just don't care. They figure they're there to do a job and if the kids don't take advantage of what they are doing then that's not their problem."

Ms. Johnson described her greatest fear in relation to David's education was teachers "not being involved."

I mean not wanting to go that extra mile. You know they're there to just do what they have to do—their curriculum—that's it. "And if you [students] don't pick it up, too bad," and there are a lot of those [teachers]. I mean just working in the school I work in, you can hear teachers all the time. It's like, "Why bother? They don't want to learn." You bother because you are supposed to bother.

Ms. Johnson "loved to death" David's 4th-grade teacher who took the class on a 3-day trip to a farm in Massachusetts. Ms. Johnson was thrilled that a teacher would be willing to do this with her class. Another teacher whose name came up in almost every interview was Mr. Lockman—David's kindergarten teacher who was stern and held high expectations, but also found unconventional ways to support children and families. As David reported, following kindergarten graduation, Mr. Lockman sent him 50 dollars, "for being a good student."

Mr. Sherwood: "Get involved"

Ms. Hollings, my teacher was strict too. She was. But she teach them, plus she was the part-time principal too. And in my time, they [would] discipline a kid. Now you can't discipline a kid the way they got it now in school . . . [when] she'd tell me to go stand in a corner, they do things. They hit you and say 'now this is what you're going to learn' and stuff. But they'll [the students will] love her for it. She was tough but fair. She was [my teacher] from 5th to 7th [grades].

Ms. Hollings' strictness and discipline—being tough, having high expectations and being fair—marked the discourse of involvement that was key to Mr. Sherwood's characterization of a good teacher. However, Mr. Sherwood's report of his strict principal/teacher must be read in conjunction with earlier memories of learning to read.

From my understanding [memory], they put like five people over here [gesturing to one side of the room] and you got one person and we got thirty kids . . . and then they have other people in the classroom [gesturing to the other side of the room]. You go in there and you try to read and stuff. They just give you the book [pause] and you supposed to read it. . . . It made me feel low 'cause the other kids were reading and I couldn't read. You know, that a hurting feeling. They taught kids and disciplined them when needed.

As Mr. Sherwood reported, with the help of his mother who took him to the public library on Saturdays and read the newspaper with him every day, he eventually learned to read. This narrative presents teachers as relinquishing their responsibility for teaching children. Rather than leaving students to learn on their own, teachers like Ms. Hollings were involved. They did not leave children to learn on their own.

When Marvin was in 5th grade, his grandfather spoke about his 4th-grade teacher: "It was just a job to her. She really didn't focus on him at all. . . . She said they just got rid of him out of the class [sent Marvin to the office]. . . . She just passed him through [to 5th grade]. . . . He didn't deserve it [his promotion to grade 5]. I mean it was terrible. Just passed him right on through—I said, 'What's this? [holding up Marvin's 4th-grade report card]. That ain't no [passing] report card.'"

Throughout the interviews, perhaps based on his experiences with Ms. Hollings, who had been both principal and teacher, Mr. Sherwood often spoke about Marvin's principals. During the year before the 5th-grade interviews, a new inexperienced assistant principal had been hired at Marvin's school. Mr. Sherwood was not pleased with the new assistant principal, "He's not really involved in a lot of things . . . so [he] won't understand what's going on." He continued, "He's got to be more active, it's a very active job, that really is." In contrast, Mr. Sherwood was pleased with the school's principal, "He got involved real good with the kids." Mr. Sherwood explained, "That's all they do is lay paperwork on him. I said, 'Man [you got to get more involved with the kids]' so he got really involved with the kids. He really did." Mr. Sherwood also reported that the principal was getting "ready to get the teachers involved."

Just as Mr. Sherwood attributed his own learning to read to his mother, he credited Marvin's grandmother with teaching Marvin to read, "Ms. Lilly when you first came to us, you know, his [Marvin's] reading skill was like [points downward] off you know, but you know what, Daisy kept reading and kept reading and kept reading [with him]. And boom! And Marvin kept going on up." As Mr. Sherwood argues, teachers need to get involved, and if they don't, parents are left to teach their children. He worries about teachers and administrators who do not work with children, promote students without making sure they have learned the necessary material, and don't get involved with students.

Ms. Rodriguez: "I can't read that"

I had one specific teacher, Mr. Grant. And he was a real good teacher. If it wasn't for him, a lot of times, I'd be sleeping in class because I was bored, and he always made it more exciting so that I could learn. . . . I was 12 when I was in his class. . . . He used to make jokes and act out a lot of those scenes and stuff. So I was like, "Okay, I can learn this. I can do this." But it was fun and then we had a lot of plays and a lot of poems that we used to read and that was interesting to me. The regular textbook wasn't interesting. It was like, "I'm going to sleep. I can't read that."

Ms. Rodriguez described how Mr. Grant made school texts more interesting by acting them out and making jokes. She complained about the "regular textbook," and in the following excerpt described the challenges her teacher faced in finding books for her and her peers in the most advanced reading group:

I was bored and she [the teacher] was trying to keep my interest but it wasn't working. . . . It's like the people in 'A' [group], it seemed like we always read everything and then she's [the teacher's] looking at us like, well I'm going up to this [other] class to get another book so you all can [read it]. That's ridiculous. Why do you go out of the classroom to keep our interest?

Both quotes highlight the importance of texts and the ways students connect with texts. In this discourse, who a student is and what that student is expected to read matter. Stopping students from being bored and keeping the students' interest is the job of the teacher. She suggested that Alicia would respond well if her teachers used music to teach reading, "If she [Alicia] combines music and puts that to words, like some words—if she can sing it then she [will] be okay. Because that's the ways she is. She can sing all the records."

When Alicia was in 1st grade, Ms. Rodriguez spoke about her older sons in high school having access to photography studios and making videos. She also suggested that teachers could use music to teach reading, "'Cause kids pick up music [more] than they pick up just regular reading. Because they [her children] can walk around here and a sing a song—more songs than I do. Some songs that I don't even know."

Ms. Mason: "It all depends on the teacher"

> Different people teach in different ways, myself for example. When I was in high school, I had psychology, and I wasn't doing that well because the teacher that I had at the time, he would explain it different, and I really didn't understand too well so when I finished school and I went to [a local business school], I had the same course again and I did great. I understand more because the instructor I had, she taught it in a way that you could understand. She gave us different examples too. I guess that it all depend on the way that person teaches.

At a later interview, Ms. Mason drew on this same example to make a point to her daughter who was in middle school at the time.

> I put my daughter for example. She just went through a lab and I heard her complain about it was boring. So I said sometimes [it] all depend on the teacher. I tell her [that] different teachers teach subjects different. Sometimes a teacher can make it more interesting for a kid and that they want to make them want to learn and then again if a teacher don't, they still think that it's boring. . . . 'Cause like for me [as an] example, when I was in high school, my last year of school I had psychology. And after I finished school then I went to [business school]. I took the same subject over again and I understood it because the teacher made it more interesting and we talked about it.

These accounts reference discourses that argue that the teacher matters. Teachers can transform boring classes and not only make them interesting but teach in ways that ensure children understand what is being taught. Her refrain was that teachers and the methods they used mattered. As a preschool teacher, Ms. Mason applied her thinking about the significance of teachers to her own work. She described strategies she has developed for engaging distracted 3-year-olds at story time.

> I have some 3-year-olds. No matter what kind of book I get they just don't have that patience and their attention span [is short] and they even get up [and walk around]. And I notice when I do a flannel board story and stuff like that, it draws all of their attention. . . . And by me doing a story [with flannels], then I let them get to touch the things, the characters, whatever [is] in that [story]. I let them touch it and that helps a lot too.

Ms. Mason highlighted the importance of engaging her students, going beyond the book to create instructional interactions that draw their attention and provide them with opportunities to interact with the materials and the story. This interest in engaging students was reflected in Javon and his goals to become a teacher. As mentioned earlier, he wanted to be a social studies teacher because he disliked social studies and thought that as a teacher he might be able "to make the kids learn to love it."

To Javon and Ms. Mason engagement is the purview of the teacher and good teachers find ways to both engage students and help them to learn material.

Ms. Holt: A teacher "who is patient"

> Ms. Thomas, she was my 3rd-grade teacher (laughs). She just pushed you to read. . . . She was hard. I mean she was hard! But she was one of those teachers, you gonna do it. You gonna do it. There's not no, I'm not going to hear the [words] "you can't" I don't believe can't was in her vocabulary. You can and you will.

This dismissal of the word *can't* recurs in Ms. Holt's advice to her children when they struggle in schools. She references a children's story about a little train engine going up the hill.

> It's like that little train—that choo-choo thing. And that little train is something else 'cause he can do it. "I can do it! I can do it!" When you put it in your mind that you can do it. You can do it. Regardless of what it is.

As Ms. Holt explains, children need a teacher "who is patient" and will work with children supporting them until they succeed. These accounts draw on discourses of patience and highlight the importance of helping children to believe that with persistence they can achieve. Ms. Holt distinguished these teachers from teachers who were inflexible and pressured students. When Bradford was in 1st grade, Ms. Holt reported that she did not enjoy reading when she was growing up, "Maybe it was that they made me read. [It was] not that enjoyable, they were trying to make me read." While she appreciated the teacher who "pushed her to read," she resented teachers "trying to make" her read.

This distinction between "I can do it" and being inflexible with students is reflected in Ms. Holt's critique of Bradford's 4th-grade teacher. She described the first time she met Ms. Douglas, "She came in [and said] 'I'm the teacher, and it's my way or no way. I'm not having no questions about any kids, nothing.'" Ms. Holt reported responding to Ms. Douglas in the following way:

Okay, I had to break it down to her. I said, "Listen here, this is not going to work.". . . She stopped that military thing where you know she had to. You know what you're doing is not working. Like I told her, "We worked too far, too hard to get Bradford where he's at for you to knock him down because of the way that you say that the lessons should be learned. All kids don't need that military style.". . . So I stopped it, I nipped it in the bud, before it got any further than this. Then me and Ms. Douglas got along very well and him and Ms. Douglas ended up doing very well. But in the beginning she had that [military style]. I'm not saying [to] baby him, but just you don't have to do him like that. Ease up a little bit. You have any problems, you call me, then we'll straighten it out. You know I don't need you to use that little military [style]. I'll do that at home.

While Ms. Holt was satisfied after this initial conversation that things would be better for Bradford, by the end of the school year she was again frustrated. She recounted her conversation with Bradford's teacher, "If you want to be honest, I tolerated her last year. I heard everything you had to say. 'Yes, okay, I'll straighten it up. Okay, Bradford, please be good. Bradford, please just go to school. Whatever the teacher tells you, just start to do [it].' [Talking on behalf of Bradford] 'But Mommy, Ms. Douglas, always picking on me.'"

Teachers making kids read and allowing children to not to read, are two sides of the same issue. It is a delicate balance between believing that children can achieve and forcing children to do things that do not make sense to them.

THOSE YOUNG TEACHERS

Age was also a factor that appeared in later interviews—perhaps because as the parents got older, their children's teachers seemed to be younger. Several parents articulated a discourse related to teacher age. As Ms. Holt reported, the teachers seemed to be getting "younger and younger." She asked, "Are they qualified to teach them or not? What's going on?"

Ms. Sherwood notes that the situation is even worse when the children are in middle and high school. She reported that some of the teachers were "still fresh out of college without really the training that they need. Like I was saying, maybe if you walk into an elementary school, that might be fine. But when you walk into the middle of a high school, fresh out of college without the training that you need, it's a difficult situation on all of them— the kids and the teacher."

Christy offered the following advice for new teachers, "You will have a hard time teaching the students a lot, 'cause they will start acting up and not listening to you 'cause you got to be more strict." David described his Math teacher who was a brand new teacher, "They [the students] do a lot of stuff to her. . . . They're always goofing. She allows them to take over."

Other students and parents reported on teachers who were small of stature who could not control their classes. David explained, "She's small, that's why they run her over. She should stop letting them run her over and send them to the office or give them detention or something."

Ms. Holt noted that being a young and inexperienced teacher might be a particular problem in urban schools. She described one of Bradford's teachers, "I try to break down some of the barriers [for him], but I'm not [sure it's working]. He's a younger teacher, Mr. Long. He can't be over 30. If he's 25, he's 25."

CONCLUSION

Ms. Horner: [Learning to read] definitely start at home. My grandmother told me [Ms. Horner laughs as she remembers] when Peter was a little baby, she says, "You say the ABCs to him, and you count to him 1 to 20 every single day, even a couple times a day, so that when he gets older, he will be up a little you know. He'll be familiar with the letters and the numbers. . . ." So that's what I did with him.

Ms. Horner's account is remarkable; the advice she shares extends across four generations. Her grandmother is Peter's great-grandmother. We witness a woman's voice impacting literacy practices across four generations. In this chapter, my goal was to situate how parents and children make sense of schooling and literacy within longitudinal familial experiences. Likewise, stories from parents' pasts are crafted in ways that inform their understandings of the present and appear to affect the ways their children interpret their own school and literacy experiences.

Critique is evident in the ways parents talk about their school experiences. As illustrated in parental accounts of *Dick and Jane*, these critiques are accompanied by nostalgic memories of texts and teachers. As Leander (2001) explains, school-related discourses are created in evolving contexts. The experiences of their children in school affect what parents remember and how parents make sense of their own school experiences. Discursive intertextuality occurs over time as parents recall texts of the past, describe favorite teachers, and draw on stories of the past to communicate with their children. The contexts in which people make sense of experiences are not static. They change and develop as people move through time and space (Leander, 2001), contributing to tensions and inconsistencies in the ways people describe their worlds. It is by grappling with this heteroglossia that people construct meanings and understandings of schools, literacies, and lives. Evolving understandings are in turn negotiated with others as people interpret their own experiences within social contexts and through socially developed discourses.

In these accounts of parents, we witness a heteroglossia of discourses relating to now-and-then, resilience, challenges of the modern world, adolescence, and youthful teachers. Some discourses about teachers focused on building relationships, doing extra things for students, getting involved, having faith in children's abilities, and how teachers teach. These discourses captured particular dimensions of teaching and tended to recur for particular speakers across interviews. Finally, artifacts of learning to read and schooling identified by parents included the *Dick and Jane* readers, SRA cards, and phonics programs, as well as computers and video technology. These artifacts evoke not only memories but meanings about schooling, literacy learning, and teachers.

CHAPTER 6

Thinking About the Future, Drawing Upon the Past, and Living in the Present

As the case studies presented in this book reveal, past, present and the future are uniquely linked in people's lives. While rarely addressed directly, this is revealed over and over again in studies that examine children's vocational aspirations. As early as 1957, Sewell, Haller, and Strauss argued that intelligence alone could not explain the educational and occupational attainment of students. The social status of families (Sewell, Haller, & Strauss, 1957), ethnic histories (Rosen, 1959), socioeconomic status (Gottfredson & Becker, 1981), gender (Bandura, Barbaranelli, Campara, & Pastorelli, 2001; Kriedberg, Butcher, & White, 1978; Looft, 1971; O'Keefe & Hyde, 1983), media experiences (Watson & McMahon, 2005), and family occupations (Schulenberg, Vondracek, & Crouter, 1984) have all been identified as important influences. While on the surface, this might appear to be a simple claim, when examined closely we note that the past histories of families contribute to status in the present and can have significant effects not only on children's futures but also on children's visions of the future. As Hartung, Porfeli, and Vondracek (2004) argue, there has been a lack of attention to the role the experiences of young children play in vocational development. Specifically, they advocate for longitudinal research that tracks vocational interests across time. As they conclude, "what children learn about work and occupations has a profound affect on the choices they make as adolescents and young adults, and ultimately, on their occupational careers" (p. 412).

In the accounts that follow, we witness participants drawing on multiple timescales including general social histories, the experiences of family members, the past experiences of family members, and envisioned futures to inform future possibilities.

WHAT DO YOU WANT TO BE WHEN YOU GROW UP?

During the first and third phases of the research project, I asked students what they wanted to be when they grew up (see Figure 6.1). The responses of the middle-schoolers indicated a rich and diverse set of goals. Many children identified vocational goals that were related to things they, or their parents, felt they did well. Bandura and his colleagues (2001) noted this in their research; as they explained, "children's perceived efficacy rather than their actual academic achievement is the key determinant of their perceived choice of worklife" (p. 187). Sometimes this ability was reported in terms of school accomplishments. Ms. Hudson reports that "Jermaine likes singing. He got As in music. In fact, the only class he got As in is music."

Several researchers (Bandura et al., 2001; Kriedberg et al., 1978; Looft, 1971; O'Keefe & Hyde, 1983) have described how gender affects students' vocational aspirations. As O'Keefe and Hyde (1983) reported, occupational stereotyping based on gender was already discernible in children at age 3, with boys tending to choose "boy jobs" and girls tending to choose "girl jobs" (p. 489). While these cultural models of gender and vocations decline as children move through elementary school and have declined historically since the woman's movement, they continue to be evident. In grade 1, all students, with the possible exception of Jermaine who wanted to be a cook, chose traditionally gendered vocations. By grade 8, most of my former students continued to identify vocations that aligned with gender stereotypes,

Figure 6.1: Vocational Aspirations

Student	Grade 1	Grades 7/8
Jermaine	cook	singer, boxer,
Christy	nurse	school secretary, state employee
David	construction worker	construction worker, builder, remodeler, athlete, small business man, business administrator, police, detective
Angela	(added to the sample in grade 5)	artist, writer, illustrator, dermagraphic artist, chemist, biologist, veterinarian, chemical engineer, web designer
Peter	soldier	photographer, artist
Bradford	police officer	caterer, vocational worker
Javon	police officer	artist, video game designer, teacher
Alicia	doctor, teacher	stepper, photographer
Marvin	police officer	auto mechanic

with a few exceptions. Only Angela chose vocations that were generally associated with the opposite gender (i.e., dermagraphic artist or tattooist, engineer, scientist). Like the choices of Jermaine, David, Javon, and Alicia, Angela's choices are disparate in the sense that she lists a wide range of occupations that require vastly different types of preparation.

In line with findings by Gottfredson and Becker (1981), the 8th-grade students' aspirations included vocations and interests that reflected family practices and occupations. Jermaine spoke of becoming a musician, explaining that his singing ability came from his "dad's side." As he noted, "My dad's a good singer. He was in a band. He played the drums." Bradford discussed the possibility of being a caterer like his mother. Marvin suspected that he would "probably fix cars"—his grandfather fixes copy machines. Javon spoke extensively about becoming a teacher—his mother taught preschool.

While David did not aspire to a job held by a family member, he did draw on a familial timescale. David attributed his interest in being a detective with memories of his father who died the summer after David was in my 1st-grade class. David recalled watching the *In the Heat of the Night* television series with his father. "I used to watch that a whole lot with my dad. Probably watch it like once a week now. I don't got my dad to watch it with [anymore]."

Similarly, Alicia's interest in being on a professional step team was intimately connected to her family. I remember her family identifying her as the "stepper" in the family and her brothers, sister, and mother gathering around to watch her perform her latest step routine in the living room. She had been on community and school step teams since elementary school. Although she was kicked off the team in middle school, she planned to try out again next year. Her other goal was to become a professional photographer which, as described below, was also connected to her role as family photographer.

The idea that parental occupations affect the choices made by children is not new. Based on their review of existing studies, Schulenberg and his colleagues (1984) maintain that specific dimensions of families (e.g., educational histories, finances, role models, informational sources) "influence specific vocational outcomes in predictable ways" (p. 139). They attribute this to the opportunities made available to children and the socialization processes that occur in the home. The following accounts highlight relationships between student aspirations and the work of parents:

- Marvin's grandfather, Mr. Sherwood, reported "He tore up something [and] I said, 'Whatcha doing, man?' and he put it right back together. I said, 'How did you do [that]?' He did it." His

> grandfather, who had attended a vocational training program, predicted, "he'll be good at that . . . . A vocational college would be the best college from him."

- By the final interview, both Ms. Mason and Javon spoke about teaching as a possible vocation. His mother noted that Javon enjoyed volunteering with the kids at the day care and sometimes played with children in the neighborhood. Javon was thinking about being a social studies teacher.

- Ms. Holt had a small catering business that she operated out of her kitchen. She noted that Bradford liked helping with the business. Ms. Holt explained that they "bring the stuff in my van and [he] brings it out . . . then he plays in the kitchen." She suspects that "when he gets of age" he might work with her. Bradford's struggles with school and the law limited his options. As Ms. Holt noted, "I have the business established . . . no telling what the future holds."

Other analyses of vocational aspiration focus on social class (Gottfredson & Becker, 1981; Bandura et al., 2001). Bandura and his colleagues (2001) challenge the assumption that vocational aspiration is linked to socioeconomic status. Instead, they argue that children's perceived self-efficacy is more significant. In other words, it is the child's belief in his or her ability to meet goals that matters more than social class or parents' income. Furthermore, they maintain that self-efficacy is linked to cultural models of gender "with boys judging themselves more efficacious for careers in science and technology and girls reporting a higher sense of efficacy for social, educational and health services" (p. 201). While the boys in my sample did not aspire to science and technological careers, they did gravitate toward gender-related occupations. (e.g., construction worker, caterer, auto mechanic, police officer). Gottfredson and Becker (1981) complicate conversations about self-efficacy noting that men tend to change or modify their vocational aspirations to match the job market and that middle class men are generally more able to fulfill their aspirations than their lower class peers. Thus they argue that self-efficacy and opportunity structures may be linked.

THEY ARE "GOOD KIDS"

Despite the fact that some of the children struggled in middle school and a few had difficulty with the law, parents maintained faith in their children. All parents invoked discourses that described their children as essentially "good kids."

Ms. Hudson: [Jermaine], he's a good child. He's just
  stubborn at times. But Jermaine is really good.
Ms. Burns: [Angela's] a good kid. She doesn't get into mischief.
Ms. Johnson: He [David] is a good kid. I couldn't ask for better.

As the students' 1st-grade teacher, I must admit that on all accounts I agreed with their assessment. One of the unique insights that accompanied conducting a longitudinal qualitative research project was observing and talking with children and families as they moved in and out of multiple spaces and situations. I have spoken with students and parents when things were going well for students and when things were not. I have heard about great accomplishments as well as significant losses, and all along the way, I have attended to how parents and children make sense of these events. In addition, like the parents, when I think about each child I invoke visions not only of the adolescent that I spoke to recently, but also the 6-year-old that I remember being in my 1st-grade class. Thus when troubles and concerns appear, parents and I share longitudinal knowledge of the potential and the talents that each child has demonstrated across time. Some parents, like Mr. Sherwood and Ms. Rodriguez, used the phrase "you know" to reference my prior knowledge of the child and his or her good qualities.

Mr. Sherwood: [Marvin's] a very gullible person. . . . But
  Marvin ain't no bad person. . . . He's a good kid, *you
  know,* he want to talk a lot of stuff but he's good.
  He's a good kid. I've got to give him that.

Similarly, Ms. Rodriguez believed that Alicia's grades were high enough and that she was heading for college. She had no major concerns about Alicia's future, noting, "[It's] just some adolescent girl stuff she's going through. *You know and I know* with her hormones . . . and thinking about boys and all that." In both cases, the use of "you know" references my longitudinal knowledge of the students. The parents remind me that I know their children and realize that despite being gullible or going through adolescence that their children are basically "good." "You know and I know" is a particularly interesting linguistic move in which Ms. Rodriguez calls upon my longitudinal knowledge of Alicia and a cultural model of what is entailed in being an adolescent to make her point.

Despite this essential faith in the students, several families recognized that situations for their children were not good. Marvin had recently been arrested for removing materials from a construction site. Mr. Sherwood was worried about how this would affect his future but maintained faith in Marvin. He reported that Marvin was trying to "maintain":

It's just, you know, right now he's adjusting to being a teenager. You know and that's all he's doing. I respect that you know. I respect that. He's not adjusting well, but he's getting there. And when he gets there he [will] be all right. He will definitely be all right.

Mr. Sherwood drew upon his own experiences and a cultural model of adolescence to assure himself of Marvin's future success. As he reported, "I used to fight; everybody has an attitude problem [when they are that age], you know?"

Marvin's essential goodness was also referenced to explain some of the difficulties Marvin has faced in school. Mr. Sherwood described Marvin's propensity to speak up when he did not agree with things at school:

Like I say, he's not no bad child. He's just want to speak his mind, you know, and the teachers don't understand that because I know the child want to speak his mind. And I know a child want to speak up and in front of certain people. You see it's hard being a teacher, because like I says, I could never be a teacher.

Mr. Sherwood sympathizes with the difficult position of teachers noting how difficult it can be to let students express their concerns while trying to teach a class. He supports Marvin's right to speak out and suggests that teachers need to understand students.

While parents retained faith in students' "goodness," sometimes parents' occupational aspirations for their children were tempered by low academic achievement and difficulties outside of school. During the initial middle school interview, Ms. Holt had predicted that Bradford might become a caterer and take over the business that she had established, but after he had been arrested, she was less confident about his future. She doubted that he would attend college explaining, "[When] he get out [of] 12th grade, he's going to say 'Hurray'. . . 'cause it's going to be so hard to get him through the 12th grade." When I asked what she thought might hold him back, Ms. Holt identified his reading abilities, "If he had better reading skills, he'd go further in life, I think. He can't read. He can't read—he don't know how."

We spoke about the possibility of enrolling him in a vocational high school. Ms. Holt agreed that this would be a good option and noted, "I'm going to [enroll him in] Job Corps before he gets disgusted." At our final interview, Ms. Holt reflected on Bradford's future:

His future is going to be totally different than I could imagine. So I have no idea what's going to happen. I have no clue. We're going to have to do this day by day, week by week. . . . I thought Bradford was going to make it to college. He was going to graduate from school. He never did really want to go to college, you know but I thought he was going to do something special . . . and it would get him on the right [track] . . . [now] I think we might, we're going to lose him.

Here we witness Ms. Holt grappling with both her faith and her fears. She juxtaposes her faith in Bradford, "I thought he was going to do something special," with her fears for his future, "I think we might, we're going to lose him."

While she was concerned about Bradford, she did not give up. She believed that his altercation with the law had drastic effects "It ran him *over* you know. Sometimes *you* need things like that. I mean a dramatic shock. [It's] terrible. You know, to get *you* back to where you're supposed to be." In this case, Ms. Holt uses the word "you" as a collective noun, referencing the effect traumatic experiences can play in helping people to get back on track. Cultural models related to being a good adolescent were referenced when she describes getting Bradford to get back to where he's "supposed to be." At the time, Ms. Holt was relieved that he was on probation and that the terms of his probation required him to stay in school. She described this probation as an opportunity for Bradford to regroup and move forward saying, "We snatched him back when he first stumped his toe."

Ms. Mason described a similar situation that occurred a couple years earlier with one of Javon's older brothers. Javon's brother had been detained by police and let off with a warning relative to drug activity in the community. As a result, Ms. Mason had a PINS (Persons in Need of Supervision) petition placed on her son. A PINS petition is filed when a parent or legal guardian seeks assistance with supervising a child. Eventually Javon's brother was sent "down south" to live with relatives and has subsequently had no further legal difficulties. She recently had a "long, long talk" with her son and recounted the conversation for my benefit. "Yeah, I said that, 'I did it in order to save you. 'Cause I knew you was a good kid and anytime you can be with the wrong group of people and something happened and sometimes a person [might] know a lot of people in jail right now for something they did not do.'"

All parents in this sample, including some who had experienced difficult times with their children, retained faith in their children's essential goodness. I argue that this faith is grounded in knowledge of the children that extends across long periods of time. While current situations might be difficult, parents draw upon past timescales, recalling children's talents, struggles in school, and past experiences. In addition, parents reference their own past histories and the challenges that accompanied being an adolescent as they defined their children as good and worthy of opportunities.

Testaments to the positive qualities of children speak to possibilities for the future. While in some cases, such as Bradford's, future options were tempered, parents retained faith in the capabilities of their children and in possibilities for the future.

TRUST IN SCHOOL

While my former 1st-grade students and their parents were often critical of schools and teachers, they placed an implicit trust in these same schools. Specifically, they had faith that schools would nurture their children's future dreams. Some scholars have written about the lack of information that low SES families have about transitioning children from high school into college (Lareau, 2003). This lack of knowledge was evident when I asked Peter if he had considered taking photography classes when he got to college. He look surprised and asked, "They have photography classes [in college]?" He then asked if he could study both art and photography—I assured him he could. In the examples below, not only is there an apparent lack of information about college, but there are also gaps in parents' knowledge about the opportunities available in local schools. Specifically, parents and children described and counted on resources that either did not exist or were inaccessible.

As described previously, Ms. Hudson reported that Jermaine was good at music. When he was in elementary school, he took a few piano lessons with his school music teacher. A professor from the local music school came to hear him play and must have been impressed because Ms. Hudson was encouraged to register Jermaine for music lessons at the local university. However, the classes were full and she never went back. In school, the only music class that Jermaine was taking was a general music class. While some children do become successful musicians without formal music training, this is rare, but Jermaine and his mother did not seem to view this lack of training as a problem. When I asked Jermaine what he needed to do to become a singer, he responded:

> [I] could do lots of stuff. I could be a singer right now if I wanted to. But I want to have an education. I could go places like sing and then later I'll do like a demo and stuff and giving it to people and if they say like do a record and stuff like that, I could do that if I want to. . . . My mom say like when American Idol Juniors come here, she going to sign me up. Me and my nephew going to get signed up 'cause my nephew sing better than me.

Similarly, Jermaine entertained equally glorious dreams of being a boxer. He explained that he had to "work out," "punch the punching bag and stuff like that," and "like if there's a boxing thing at my school, I could do that. And you can get a scholarship and stuff like that." While Jermaine described strategies for becoming a boxer—working out and punching the bag—he was not sure whether his school offered boxing opportunities, and generally referenced a "scholarship and stuff like that." Other students and their families made comments that revealed a possible lack of awareness of the processes that might lead to future goals.

On several occasions, Alicia spoke of becoming a photographer. While Alicia complained that her school did not have a photography club, her mother assured her that there would be photography classes and a photography club when she got to high school. "They have stuff that they will help her do [it]. She'll learn how to develop pictures and stuff like that." However, reviewing data collected when Alicia was in high school, these courses and clubs were not available.

Dreams of becoming a photographer were also complicated by Alicia's limited experiences. Specifically, Alicia had only used disposable cameras, "I be getting those little small plastic cameras and take pictures of everybody and stuff." Luckily, her uncle worked for a company that processed film from the disposable cameras; he would develop her pictures and include a CD. She described using her computer to modify one of the pictures by "putting all kinds of things" in the picture. Alicia had also read information on the Internet about taking good pictures, and wanted to eventually take pictures of "flowers, people, landscapes, water—things like that."

Despite these limited experiences, Alicia was confident in both her ability and her prospects. She reported, "Yeah, I'm [a] good [photographer]." While Alicia realized that professional cameras were expensive, she assured me, saying, "I know my mom will get it . . . 'cause she already told me she's going to give me like one of them photography cameras." Alicia suspected that she will "probably try to get in college," and that she has to "just try to do your best, try to fixate on what you want to do."

Interestingly, Alicia's and her mother's faith in school was contradicted by the experiences of Alicia's older brother. Tyreek had been in my 1st-grade class several years before I taught Alicia. He was one of the brightest students I have ever taught and was a brilliant reader. Unfortunately, in high school, Tyreek got into trouble and was placed in a special class for students who misbehaved in school. Ms. Rodriguez explained, "He don't like it 'cause it's only like one or two people in the classes with him so you know he don't want to be there. . . . He's bored." I asked if the teachers were giving Tyreek challenging work that would prepare him for college.

Ms. Rodriguez shook her head, noting that Tyreek wanted to "become an engineer and he loved computers," but she doubted that the program he was in would prepare him for college.

Faith in school was evident across the sample. Ms. Johnson was confident that business classes would be available when David got to high school. Javon believed that the computer class he had taken last year would help to prepare him to become an artist and a video game designer. He had not taken art courses since elementary school. Mr. Sherwood and Ms. Holt both spoke about sending their sons to vocational high schools but neither was clear on what programs were available.

Angela and her mother were the only participants in the sample who seemed to have a clear plan for college. Angela was also the only student who was currently living with parents who had graduated from 2-year colleges. While she described a wide range of possible career interests—ranging from chemistry to writing to being a dermagraphic (tattoo) artist. Angela and her mother agree that Angela would attend the local community college for two years and then transfer to a private four-year school. As Ms. Burns explained to her daughter and me, the first two years will cost half as much and "you still get the same degree from the 4-year school."

Looking forward to the high school interviews, it is apparent that Jermaine did not participate in music classes and there were no opportunities at school for boxing. Photography classes were not available for Alicia, and David did not find the business classes he envisioned. Students complained about high schools with crumbling buildings, tattered textbooks, and no football teams. Only Marvin found the vocational education courses that he sought.

MAINTAINING DREAMS

In the literature on occupational aspiration, there is a category of "fantasy professions" identified by young children (Trice, 1991, p. 138). These professional aspirations include becoming a "clown" or a "princess" and generally dissipate as children grow older. Trice reports that by age 8 only 2% of children still report these types of goals. Although in middle school Angela joked about possibly becoming a vampire, by age 11, as Trice reported, none of the students in my study offered fantasy responses. The dreams presented in this section are clearly not the same as these childlike fantasy professions; however, they do point to remarkable possibilities. I do not argue that these dreams are not possible. In fact each one presents hope as well as real-life possibilities and promises.

Jermaine described how his family would tease him about the possibility that he would not graduate from high school. Jermaine recreated his response:

> "How do you know I'm not going to graduate from high school? When I prove [to] you I finish school and I get a good job and I be famous that going to prove that y'all stupid. Now y'all going to look stupid [and] be asking me for some money. But they looked in my eyes and they went, 'You're not going to have money. You're going to be [a] low n-_____-r on the street.' I say, 'Keep on thinking that. When I stay in college and do all I got to do and be all famous, don't be coming begging me for some money.' So I'm like 'You're the stupid one now.'"

Jermaine's account is complex. While it could read as a response to cruel interaction that situated him as a hopeless student, knowing this family for the past 7 years and being particularly aware of the commitment his mother and father have made to Jermaine's education, I believe that in this incident, his family members were strategically baiting Jermaine, demanding that he verbalize, defend, and embody his intention of staying in school. As Jermaine explained, the primary instigator was his 32-year-old brother, who regretted not graduating from high school. Jermaine's brother forced him to defend his intention to complete school and to consider the pride that he could eventually take in this accomplishment. Notably, Jermaine took on and performed this interaction for me, his 1st-grade teacher—defending his intention to complete high school, attend college, get a good job, and support himself. Jermaine's positioning was grounded in the histories of family members—mother, father, and brother who did not graduate from high school and a sister who, despite the challenges of being a single mother, earned a college degree—proving that college was a possibility for Jermaine.

Over the course of the middle school interviews, Jermaine shared other performances related to the future. In addition to being selected for American Idol, he described his plans to become a boxer:

> I gonna have to get my hands licensed. 'Cause I hit too hard. I hit harder than these grown people. I do and I'm stronger than them too. That's why I don't be trying like to fight. 'Cause the last person I fought, I cracked his head open because I was mad. I was real mad. I hit him one good time in the head and his head was just nasty.

While among the students in the sample, Jermaine's accounts were probably the most graphic and entertaining, other students and parents also presented dreams of glory. Ms. Johnson reported, "when he's [David's] rich and famous he's going to buy me a mansion." While David was interested in business and often spoke of becoming wealthy, he also dreamed of becoming a detective. Despite his mother's preference for David going into business because "no one respects the police," David was enthusiastic about detective work. He described his plan, saying that "as soon as the police go down the street they [the kids hanging out on the streets], doing the same things again." As he reported, "I got a trick for that. I could set up cameras. I'm going to make a protest about that. I'm going to have my research be setting up [a] camera on all of the major drug places and some of the finer places [where] they buy their clothes."

In terms of business possibilities, David noted that he might either own his own business or work for a corporation. He named a national corporation located in the area saying, "I think I could help them. Once I get down [to work], start cracking the books. . . . I could help them a lot." David's goals were tied to his family, "Get a job [and] keep it steady to get a nice house and seeing [to it that] my mom's still in good condition and all that stuff and get her a nice car, stay loyal, stay respectful."

Peter had dreams of spending the summer after his last year of high school abroad. I have used his responses to my questions to craft the following description:

> After my last year of high school, in the summer, I want to do like travel and be a photographer and things. And then I'll try to go to college and study art. I think it's cool. I want to go mostly in Europe and you know take lots of pictures and meet a whole bunch of different kinds of people. I'd take pictures of the sights and the things that are most famous about that country. I'll probably sell them to a newspaper or something.

He later described working hard in school so that he could "skip to the next grade" and be able to graduate with his two best friends. They were hoping to spend their senior year in high school as exchange students in Japan.

Finally, Ms. Holt described a dream that was actually coming true for Bradford's older brother who was attending college on a tennis scholarship. "I am so proud of my son. In January he's going pro. Reebok offered him 20 million for 3 years. But if he takes that he has to withdraw [from college] and I think go to Florida." She explained that while her son was hesitant about leaving school, other family members encouraged him to take the offer:

> They were pulling him and pulling him, do this, do this. I said, "I trust you in this matter. You decide what you want to do. Whatever you

think is best for you, that's what you do. . . ." 'Cause his grandmother and all told him you stop going to college, go for it, go for it, go for it. But he just sat down and he told me what he wanted, and I said, "Do whatever you want to do."

Bradford's brother turned down the offer, but finished college with a degree in physical education and coaching. He is now a tennis coach at an exclusive resort.

As I reflect on the vocational aspirations of my former students, I consistently experience troubling emotions. Do I believe that Jermaine will prove his family wrong and become famous? Will he become a champion boxer or appear on American Idol? Will David become a policeman and use his ingenuity to make the streets in his community safe? Will he become a successful businessman working with a major corporation? Will Peter and his friends travel to Japan and Europe? After all, dreams were coming true for Bradford's brother. However, the demographics of students in this city suggest that completing high school, attending college, and becoming financially successful is not the norm for people from this low-income community. At the time of my research, only about 50% of the students from the local school district graduated high school.

Literature on vocational attainment explores race, socioeconomic status, and gender—three variables that appear to affect vocational attainment. When discussing race and ethnicity, it is essential to recognize that the ways racial and ethnic categories are currently constructed are very different from the ways they were conceptualized in the past. In 1959, Rosen wrote a paper exploring the achievement orientations of six racial and ethnic groups: French Canadians, Southern Italians, Greeks, East European Jews, "Negros," and U.S.-born White Protestants—which he describes as the "most heterogeneous" (p. 49). While these may seem like unusual categories to a contemporary reader, Rosen articulated clear expectations for each group. For example, he referenced the classic work of Max Weber to support his claim that "the most important aspects of the Protestant theological position was the shift from reliance on an institution (the church) to a greater reliance on self" (p. 50) and noted that "the observation that Jews stress achievement training is commonplace" (p. 51). In contrast, he reported "surprisingly" (p. 56) that "83% of the Negro (much higher than was anticipated)" mothers expected their sons to go to college (p. 58).

Then as now, race and class play a role in vocational attainment. Unavoidable complications accompany being Black, biracial, Latino, and poor. Just as Rosen's report reveals the stereotypes that were brought to discussions of achievement orientation in 1959, current assumptions and beliefs circulate today and affect the ways children are educated and supported as they move from educational institutions into the workforce.

CONCLUSION

The vocational aspirations of students are constructed within contexts that involve cultural models of gender and occupations alongside experiences within families. Despite the challenges that many families faced, parents were adamant in positioning their children as *good kids* and invited me to confirm this assessment. Discourses related to being a teenager were often voiced. In tension with their own experiences and the experiences of their older children, parents maintained a notable trust in school that was generally broken when the students arrived in high school and were not provided with the experiences they expected. Like their parents, the middle school students held tight to dreams of possible futures.

CHAPTER 7

Time and Literacy Practices: Becoming a Reader Over Time

When Alicia was in 1st grade, her mother, Ms. Rodriguez, described her own experiences in high school. "School wasn't for me. To me it was boring. It was so boring I used to go to sleep." Eight years later, when I asked Alicia about the worst part of school, she told me, "Going to sleep in class in the morning." When I asked her if she really slept in class, Alicia responded, "Yeah, when my teacher's boring."

When Alicia was in 1st grade, I asked her mother why some people never learn to read; she explained, "A lot of them just figured school wasn't for them. They just dropped out." Eight years later when I asked Alicia why she thought that the kids at school don't like to read, she told me, "'Cause they just not into it."

When Alicia was in 1st grade, I asked her mother why she liked to read. Ms. Rodriguez responded, "It takes you to a different place. It relaxes you." Eight years later, Alicia told me, "I just like it [reading]; it can take my mind away from things."

What is the significance of mother and daughter expressing the same ideas in almost the same words 8 years apart? Is the similarity in their comments simply because they are both accessing commonplace ways of talking about schooling and literacy? Or is the similarity due to the transfer of certain ways of being, valuing, and knowing across generations? In this chapter I will argue that both Ms. Rodriguez's and Alicia's explanations involve time and the construction of ways of being, valuing, and knowing across time. People construct meanings over time as similar messages recur. People also construct various meanings at different times, drawing on available discourses, shared cultural models, and familial and historical meanings.

When Alicia was in grade 8, Ms. Rodriguez was a 42-year-old single mother. She had six children—four older sons (Tyreek, Leon, James, and P.T.) and two daughters (Alicia and her younger sister Quanzaa). Leon had grown-up and moved out of state. James, P.T., and Tyreek were in high school. It was while I was reading transcripts and field notes from Alicia's case in conjunction with themes identified in the larger project that I realized how her case could provide a lens for illustrating temporal dimensions of literacy, identity, and race. This is attributable to three factors: the propensity of Alicia, her mother, and her siblings to address a range of issues that included sensitive topics (i.e., race, social class); Ms. Rodriguez's extensive experiences with literacy and schooling; and the tendency for various family members to interject their thoughts and ideas into the interviews.

I draw on Alicia's story to examine identity construction as readers move through time and through school. I apply the construct of timescales (Lemke, 2000, 2001; Wortham, 2006) to document the ways one student and her family members contextualized their experiences in ways that were both recursive and future-oriented, referencing ongoing experiences and familial and historical resources, while constructing themselves as readers and people. I also draw on critical race theory (Ladson-Billings & Tate, 1995), and specifically the construct of counter-stories (Solórzano & Yosso, 2002), which reflect alternative discourses that challenge generally accepted understandings of the world. These stories are grounded in people's life experiences and reveal complexities and nuances of experience that are often not reflected in dominant discourses. Temporal experiences that draw on history alongside family stories are particularly significant for students, like Alicia, who are members of communities that historically have not been well-served by schools. By attending to time, educators can begin to recognize students as agents who draw upon available resources at multiple timescales to make sense of their worlds and their roles in these worlds. As described in Chapter 1, Lemke (2000, 2001, 2005) uses the construct of timescale to capture the multiple ways people operate within time and to explore the multiple temporal worlds they inhabit and the meanings they construct.

In this chapter I first present case study data to illustrate the ways Alicia and her family members draw upon family histories and larger social histories as they make sense of their world and literacy practices. Second, I document Alicia as an active agent who accesses available resources at multiple timescales to pursue her interests. Finally, I examine the complexity of identity construction over time.

SCHOOL, RACE, AND ALICIA'S FAMILY

This first set of stories highlights schooling and race and draws explicitly on familial and historical timescales. Within this set of stories, I present counter-stories related to language, attending urban schools, and teachers. These stories illustrate how larger social histories that involve inequities in American society impact Alicia's ongoing and familial experiences. Specifically, these counter-stories have roots in racism, classism, and the history of urban schooling. These stories were shared within the family over long periods of time and contributed to the ways people in this family make sense of themselves and their worlds.

Stories Related to Language

Ms. Rodriguez and her children are speakers of African American Language. After her mother died, Ms. Rodriguez was raised by an aunt. When Alicia was in my 1st-grade class, Ms. Rodriguez recalled questioning her aunt about the ways she spoke at home and school. She recounted the following story:

> When she used to come to school she'd say, "Just, you know" [spoken with a polite intonation] and I'm sitting there like [Ms. Rodriguez has an expression of amazement on her face]. "Wait a minute, Aunt, that ain't the same way you talk to us when we be home." And her's like, "No, no, no, no. This is different." So when she explained it I was like, "Okay." So, when I'm out in that street I can say, "Yo, what's up." But when I get downtown [at the city school district offices] and I'm in front of everybody you know and I'm dressed, it's "Hi, how are you doing?" and "Well, I'm here for so and so."

Ms. Rodriguez draws on cultural models that privilege what is known as standard English as she discusses the African American English spoken by members of her family. Ms. Rodriguez's account highlighted the differences in the ways her aunt spoke at home and at school. She used the anecdote to illustrate the lessons her aunt taught her about language and the way this lesson continues to affect her interactions with teachers and administrators. The distinctions her aunt made were valuable and important. They challenge dominant discourses that denigrate the language of speakers of African American Language and highlight the linguistic facility of African American people.

In a second account, also told when Alicia was in 1st grade, Ms. Rodriguez described conveying this same message to her own children. She recounted testing her teenage boys to make sure they could talk "proper" by sending them to speak with people on the street who she believed were speakers of privileged forms of English. She eavesdropped on their conversations to assess their language and interaction skills. Ms. Rodriguez explained that she was glad that her sons could "make that conflict" between African American language and privileged forms of English because it would be "easier for them."

Ms. Rodriguez demonstrates agency and control in a situation that could be disempowering. Her linguistic competencies are evident, and just as her aunt explicitly shared her competencies, Ms. Rodriguez passed these lessons on to her children. While dominant discourses might deny the linguistic competencies of speakers of African American English, Ms. Rodriguez challenges dominant discourses by demonstrating her linguistic insights and ability.

Stories Related to Attending Urban Schools

The second set of stories involved issues related to attending urban schools. The school where Alicia attended 1st grade was located in a low-income area of the city. It was bordered on two sides by housing projects that had been built following a series of race riots during the 1960s. Although, Alicia and her family did not live in the projects, Ms. Rodriguez draws upon cultural models of a ghetto to describe her community. The following story reflected Ms. Rodriguez's concerns about living in the ghetto and having her children attend urban schools:

A lot of teachers in a lot of schools . . . they say this is the ghetto, right? And they say a lot of people is in the ghetto so they assume everybody is on welfare. And they'll say "When your mother get her check, tell her to buy you so and so." And that's embarrassing for the kid.

Ms. Rodriguez identified teachers as being susceptible to assumptions about people who lived in this poor community. She explained that these assumptions led teachers to make class-based comments that could embarrass children. Basically, the teacher had told Quanzaa to make sure that her mother bought her new gloves when she got her welfare check. In contrast to this dominant account that characterized poor African American parents, like Ms. Rodriquez, as uncaring and negligent, Ms. Rodriguez presented a counter-story. She recounted going to the school and explaining to Quanzaa's teacher that she realized that Quanzaa had lost her gloves. Ms. Rodriguez allowed Quanzaa to wear her own gloves when she walked to school; when they arrived at school, Ms. Rodriguez reclaimed her gloves and walked to work. Quanzaa was picked up by a neighbor who drove her home after school and thus did not need the gloves. Ms. Rodriguez voiced a counter-story of resourcefulness challenging dominant discourses of neglect about low-income parents.

A second set of counter-stories were shared when Alicia was in 5th grade, Ms. Rodriguez explained that when she was in high school she witnessed students being allowed to progress through school without learning:

See, I come from New York. So, with us it's, in New York a lot of times you slip through that system and you just skid. The kids get pushed through school without learning anything. And I *refuse* to let that happen to mine. *I refuse it!* And it got to the point where even when we got up here, you have to be that parent that actually cares and let them know that you care and let them know they're not going to push your child through school.

Ms. Rodriguez's repeated emphasis placed on the word *refuse* accentuates her message. She described the importance of agency by letting school personnel know that she did care, because school personnel "figure most of the time the Black kids, a lot of them, they have a parent that don't care, so you have to actually show them that 'Uh-uh, no, this is a parent that do care.'" She explained that she would "write letters, show up at school meetings, and talk to the teachers" to ensure that her children were well served.

Five months later, Ms. Rodriguez expressed a similar opinion; again she named race as a critical factor in the ways students are treated in schools: "My point of view is more or less more that if you're White, it seems like you get a better education but a Black person a lot of times they just try to push you through school, and which I refuse to have to them push my kids through school." Ms. Rodriguez highlighted her role as an advocate for her children and spoke back to dominant discourses by claiming agency as an African American mother and acting on behalf of her children.

A third set of stories referenced teachers. When Alicia was in 8th grade, she reported that whether she was polite to teachers depended on "how the teacher be acting towards you. If you act mean towards me, I'm acting mean back. If you act nice I'm acting nice back." She added that her school was "not really" a good place to learn. Alicia faulted the teachers for not maintaining control in their classrooms and maintained that her peers often frightened their teachers. Alicia's mother shared her concerns about teachers; she described a time when her youngest daughter, Quanzaa, got in trouble with her teachers.

For every little thing, I mean every little thing they [get suspended]. . . . Quanzaa got suspended last year. Because I told her to wait outside for her ride. And they talk about she couldn't wait outside. She had to wait in the ISS room [in-school suspension]. I said "No, I told her to wait here. You can't tell her something different because all that's going to do is upset her." She got suspended for it. Talking about she was talking back. And all she was doing was trying to tell them, "My mother told me to wait here."

In this story, teachers were described as unwilling to listen to the students and unaware of how children were caught between their parent's instructions and school policies.

At various points in the interviews, both Alicia and her mother reported that teachers were just there "for a paycheck." In contrast to depictions of urban teachers as saintly and altruistic, Ms. Rodriguez and Alicia described teachers as uncaring, distant, unreasonable, fearful, and unresponsive to their students. These depictions draw on counter-stories that reflected their own experiences and the experiences of family members.

Considering Counter-Stories

Three types of counter-stories, each challenging a different assumption about poor African American families, were evident in the data sets presented above. First, rather than ascribing to dominant discourses that portray speakers of African American language as unsophisticated, Ms. Rodriguez's words conveyed knowledge about language use and power. She presented a thorough understanding of the role language plays in multiple social contexts, described her aunt as conveying this information to her, and reported passing these insights on to her children. Second, counter-stories challenged the assumption that schools provided all students with equitable educational opportunities. Ms. Rodriguez identified both race and social class as factors that affected her children's educational experiences. She portrayed herself as active in demanding that her children were well served by their schools. Finally, counter-stories challenged portrayals of urban teachers as committed and caring individuals who were not successful with their students because students' families were uninvolved and uninterested. Both Alicia and Ms. Rodriguez described incidents in which teachers were unresponsive to their students. Yet in urban schools that serve poor communities, the status quo involves policies that sustain underfunded urban school systems, resulting in overwhelmed and overworked teachers, and reductive and irrelevant textbook-driven curricula. These counter-stories challenged dominant discourses (Solórzano & Yosso, 2002) about language, urban families, and schooling. In this analysis, I am not concerned with the *truthfulness* of the counter-stories; the importance of the narratives lay in their contribution to the ways of being, knowing, and valuing that have informed Alicia's evolving identity construction and contribute to her relationships with schooling and literacy over long periods of time.

Counter-stories related to schooling and race involved events that occurred within the family and continued to affect the family. The stories circulate across familial timescales—the past influencing the present, the present affecting the ways people make sense of the past, and the past and the present contributing to conceivable futures. Because family members often contributed to these stories by providing missing details and expanding on each another's comments, I suspect that these stories were told prior to my visits and were told long after my visits ended. While they were recounted in the lived present, these stories described events and experiences from the familial past in ways that denied simple linear processes. Stories from different times and places co-occurred, intermingled, and were accessed in a nonchronological manner. The stories were recursive as participants revisited stories and events that occurred years apart—stories of getting "pushed through school" told when Alicia was in 5th grade were echoed in 8th grade. Ms. Rodriguez's insights about language connected to her aunt were re-enacted in her own interactions with her sons as they become young men. As illustrated in the introduction to this chapter, Alicia and her mother used almost identical words, 8 years apart as they spoke about school and literacy. Alicia and her siblings learned important lessons about race and society as they confronted historically constructed, inequitable, and racially biased situations.

The stories told in Alicia's family also drew on historical timescales and reflected larger histories of racism and classism in America. When Ms. Rodriguez told stories about the use of language in official contexts, she referenced formidable and historically embedded timescales that have systematically privileged White, middle and upper class forms of English over African American English. When Ms. Rodriguez named the assumptions made by teachers about families in the ghetto, she did not confront merely an individual teacher, she confronted a dominant discourse about poor urban parents that had deep roots in American social history. Being pushed through school without learning was not a concern unique to members of this family; it was a historical practice connected to underfunded and understaffed schools, deficit assumptions about the learning capabilities of African American students, and the systemic under-education of generations of African American students in the United States (Auerbach, 1989; Jencks & Phillips, 1998; Rist, 1978). Stories of language discrimination, assumptions based on economic disparity and race, and dysfunctional relationships between teachers and students were not exclusive to Alicia's family; they are endemic and historically pervasive in the lives of African American people. As Alicia made sense of her world, she referenced historic accounts that continue to contribute to her ways of being and her understandings of the world. Alicia witnessed the role race played in the lives of family members, and as illustrated in the following section, race became salient in Alicia's literacy practices.

Despite the power of historic and familial ways of understanding the world, Alicia did not passively construct her understanding of the world. Neither the perspectives of her mother, or her brothers, or her little sister inscribed Alicia with particular views. Alicia's understandings of the world incorporated experiences that challenged and complicated meanings that circulated at the familial timescale. In contrast to her mother's use of the word *ghetto,* Alicia, as described later in this chapter, used the word *ghetto* to describe her 5th-grade teacher as "cool." Despite her mother's critique of teachers, for most of the time I knew Alicia, she was an A and B student and liked most of her teachers. In addition, the close relationship I shared with Alicia over the past 10 years challenged her family's characterization of teachers as uncaring. There were tensions between Alicia's understanding of the world and the counter-stories told by her mother and brothers. All of school was not negative, and the family's readings of race and schooling were neither consistent nor uniform.

READING PRACTICES IN ALICIA'S FAMILY

While participating in historical, familial, and ongoing timescales, Alicia constructed her own relationships to schooling and her own understandings of herself as a young African American woman within a particular set of discourses, relationships, and experiences. In the following section, I present three data sets related to literacy in Alicia's family and Alicia's literacy practices. Specifically I present data related to Ms. Rodriguez's childhood memories of reading at home and school, ongoing reading practices in Alicia's home, and Alicia's reading practices in grades 1, 5, and 8. These data sets illustrate how familial literacy practices are exchanged and individualized.

Ms. Rodriguez's Childhood Reading Practices

Ms. Rodriguez traced her love of reading to her mother. She laughed as she recounted her memories:

> When I first learned to read, my mother taught me. And she was teaching me the ABCs and stuff like that, and she was teaching me words. But she wasn't teaching me the small words like *it* and *is* and *the.* So when I learned how to read, I learned the big words, and then when she used to always tell me to read to her, it was like "How come you know all the

big words?" I said, "That's what you taught me. You didn't teach me the small ones." (laughs) That's [the way it was], and it was fun because it was doing something different, and I always like a challenge.

Reflecting documented literacy practices in African American families (Compton-Lilly, 2003; Gadsden, 2005; Lanehart, 2002), Ms. Rodriguez identified her mother as the person who taught her to read and remembered learning to read as "fun." She brought interest, engagement, and enthusiasm to reading.

When I asked Ms. Rodriguez about reading at school, she described a favorite 7th-grade English teacher,

> He used to make jokes and act out a lot of those scenes [from books] and stuff, so it was like, "Okay, I can learn this. I can do this." But it was fun and then we had a lot of plays and a lot of poems that we used to read and that was interesting to me. The regular textbook wasn't interesting. It was like going to sleep. . . . Them books [that they gave us to read in school] was soooo easy and I used to breeze through them . . . . [The teacher would ask] "So what are you up to?" I'm like "You don't want to know. Can I get another book?"

Again, reading was described as "fun"; however, like Alicia and her peers, as described in Chapter 3, Ms. Rodriguez made a clear distinction between reading authentic texts and reading the "regular textbook" which "wasn't interesting." She remembered learning to read as easy and described herself as moving quickly through the texts assigned by her English teacher. She explained, "See personally I liked novels and stuff like that, so if [you] want to make a child read just give them something that they like to read."

Agency, engagement, and enjoyment characterize Ms. Rodriguez's reading practices. Just as her mother shared these practices with her, as described in the following section, Ms. Rodriguez fosters literacy practices with her children.

The Family's Literacy Practices

Ms. Rodriguez brought a rich set of literacy practices to her children. She demonstrated agency in her efforts to help her children. Throughout the interviews, Ms. Rodriguez described herself as an avid reader, "All of my friends are good readers, all of them." She reported, "We like to trade [books]." Ms. Rodriguez laughed as she recreated a conversation with one of her friends:

Ms. Rodriguez: Got a good novel?
Friend: Ahhhhh, did you read so and so, so and so? No?
Ms. Rodriguez: You got it?
Friend: Yeah. You should check it out.
Ms. Rodriguez: Send it by so and so, or I come and get it.

Literacy practices, friendships, and books intersect as Ms. Rodriguez enacts her identity as reader. Ms. Rodriguez spoke extensively about the importance of supporting her children as readers and her expectation that her children would also value reading. "My kids started reading from the beginning. I read to them and by me reading to them they wanted to read. So I figure that's probably the type of child that [they] will grow up [to be]."

In addition, Ms. Rodriguez believed that Alicia's brothers played a significant role in Alicia's development as a reader. "When she's reading along, she comes to me. And if she don't come to me she goes to one of her brothers. And we told her the same thing. 'Sound it out!'" Alicia confirmed her mother's account that her brothers helped her and assured me that she planned to help her little sister with reading, "I want to help her listen to the words." While dominant discourses about sounding out words as the key to reading are evident in these data, the active role of family members, and particularly Alicia's brothers, is apparent. Learning to read is a responsibility that extends beyond the child and her parent, and includes family members who work together to ensure literacy learning.

When Alicia was in 5th grade, Ms. Rodriguez identified Donald Goines as her favorite author. She explained, "He is a Black author. . . . He write about his life and about different parts of his life. The last one I read was *White Man's Justice, Black Man's Grief*" (Goines, 1973). She was currently reading a book by Terry McMillan entitled *Mama* (1987) that she had gotten from one of her girlfriends.

> My girlfriend said, "She [the protagonist] reminds me of you in some ways" and I was like, when I started reading that, I called her up and I said "Roneta, no, uh-uh. She don't remind you of me. Home girl [the main character in the story] is a whore." [Roneta responded] "No, I am talking she got five kids." I am like "Oh, okay. That part yeah but you know, a whore?"

Ms. Rodriguez's enthusiasm for reading extended to her children, "I just finished reading that [Ms. Rodriguez pointed to the book, *Mama*] now Leon reading it." When I returned for the next interview, Leon had also finished reading *Mama* and was looking for a new book to read. He reported, "I need more books. That's why I called Roneta." Leon told me that in school he had read *The Taming of the Shrew* (Shakespeare, 2004), *A*

Rose for Emily (Faulkner, 1931/2007), and *A Raisin in the Sun* (Hansberry, 1958/2002). He identified Shakespeare as his favorite writer.

Reading practices and preferences both varied and overlapped. Leon's brothers primarily read magazines, including *Sports Illustrated* and various music magazines. During Alicia's 5th-grade year, Tyreek brought a biography of Martin Luther King home from school and Ms. Rodriguez read it aloud to Alicia and Quanzaa. The books Tyreek was reading included some from the *Goosebumps* Series (Stine, 1992–1997), which Alicia and Quanzaa also reported reading in later interviews.

Alicia's Reading Practices in Grade 1

During my first visit to Alicia's home, Ms. Rodriguez showed me a huge box of books that she had been collecting since her boys were little. The box was obviously well-used, and the entire family gathered around to view the books. Inside were board books, Little Golden Books, Dr. Seuss books, discarded library books, and old school textbooks; many of the books were old and tattered. At his mother's request, Tyreek brought out 20 books from his bedroom and exchanged them for books from the box. His older brother, Leon, who was about 13 years old, asked for all the Dr. Seuss books. Ms. Rodriguez told him "No" explaining that he was too old for Dr. Seuss. Another older brother, P.T., got his social studies textbook and offered it to Tyreek to read. Tyreek accepted the book readily (From fieldnotes 1-4-97). In my 1st-grade fieldnotes, I compared Alicia to her older brother, Tyreek:

> Alicia is more social than her brother and does not always focus [on the books] when she reads. Reading is a more social experience. She is a leader in the classroom and generally spends her independent reading time at a table with three other girls reading books together. When they finish, they get up as a group and select a new title bringing it back to their table and reading it chorally (Fieldnotes 1-2-97).

Alicia had many friends in our 1st-grade classroom and enjoyed reading and writing activities especially if they involved working with peers. Like many of the students in 1st grade, Alicia identified schoolbooks as her favorites and named titles from our classroom library. Alicia believed that she was a good reader because she could read many books independently.

Alicia's Reading Practices in Grade 5

When Alicia was in 5th grade, I asked about her favorite books at school. She answered, "None," but explained that she had read eight of the books in *The Baby-sitter's Club* Series (Martin & Lerangris, 1986–2000).

She explained that her teacher did not assign these books, but she chose to read them in school at silent reading time. I asked Alicia if there were any Black characters in the Baby-sitter's books. She told me that there were but she could not remember their names. When asked if it was important that books have Black characters, Alicia shook her head, "no." Mackey (1990) argues that these books present a "token multiculturalism," despite the presence of African American characters in the books, "every character speaks from the perspective of the White middle-class white" (p. 486). In addition to the Baby-sitter's books, Alicia also read books by Judy Blume, and still enjoyed her childhood *Winnie the Pooh* books. At the time of the interview, she was reading a biography of David Robinson, an African American basketball player.

Alicia and I discussed some of the books that were assigned in school; she named *There's an Owl in the Shower* (George, 1997) and *The Cry of the Crow* (George, 1988), but told me that *Two Under Par* (Henke, 2005) was her favorite. When asked about the plot of the story, Alicia responded, "I don't know." In response to my prompting she described only the opening scene of the book saying that she could not remember any more. Alicia enjoyed writing in school and explained that she and her classmates were collaborating to write scenes for a play.

Alicia's Reading Practices in Grade 8

By 8th grade, Ms. Rodriguez reported that Alicia never brought books home from school and never visited the local library. She explained, "Alicia's more interested in how she looks now. . . . She won't go outside with her hair undone. Clothes got to be okay." Ms. Rodriguez assured me that she was not worried about Alicia, "'Cause I know that's just teenagers who want to be with the in-people."

In 8th grade Alicia's class studied *The Tell-Tale Heart* (Poe, 1983) in English class. As reported in Chapter 3, she complained that "It's kinda boring" and "It ain't scary," but later clarified that she thought the way her teacher read the text aloud to the class was boring. I asked if they were doing any other reading in school; Alicia responded, "We ain't doing nothing."

While Alicia no longer brought books home from school, she was reading. Ms. Rodriguez reported that at home Alicia was reading, "Those novel things—love novels." When she sent Alicia to get the book she was reading, Alicia emerged from her bedroom with a book about an African American teenager entitled *Ruby* (Guy, 1991). Alicia explained that she had not yet started it and that she had "stole it" from her brother. Alicia said that she generally got her books from her mother, who got the books from friends, "then she read them, then I take them and I read them." Alicia explained that the books she read were "grown-up books" and "mostly about sex"; they featured African American characters. While at one point in the interview Alicia said that her friends sometimes read magazines, she later reported that when she was with her friends, "We don't read nothing." Ms. Rodriguez told me, "Alicia can read her little tail off," and explained that the "last time we checked her reading we was on 10th-grade level."

Ms. Rodriguez reported that Alicia also wrote poetry. When I asked Alicia to read one of her poems into my tape recorder, she readily agreed and disappeared into her room returning with a tattered notebook and read several poems (see Figure 7.1). Alicia explained that she wrote these poems while she was visiting her brother in Virginia. She could not explain how she learned to write poetry, saying, "I just started."

Figure 7.1: Alicia's Poems

Angel

One day I'm gonna have some one I can hold.
Some one who can be at my side 24/7
Even if I want them to hug me at the 7-11.
I want someone who can kiss me hi and bye.
I want some one who won't hurt me and die.
God, can you give me someone who has skin as soft as a baby.
I want you to give me some one who smells like a daisy.
I want someone who's not fragile.
That someone will be my angel.

Hate

Hey, there's a person that I ain't, can't stand.
And they will never be my friend.
Sometimes they can hurt my feelings.
It don't matter because I can always take the hurt away by writing.
No, I can't take the pain.
I'm gonna need a cane cause because I'm gonna break my leg.
Because all of the pain.
That's why this person I will always hate.

Discussion of Alicia's and the Family's Reading Practices

These stories of reading in Alicia's family challenge dominant discourses about reading in poor African American families. While people tend to characterize urban families as illiterate or alliterate, these stories describe an

African American family that engages in a range of literacy practices. Echoing findings from research conducted by Gadsden (2005) and Lanehart (2002), while many African American homes feature rich and meaningful literacy practices, these practices may not consistently reflect school expectations.

Familial timescales provide a lens for considering family literacy practices over time. Ms. Rodriguez's commitment to helping her children become readers reflects her own reading experiences with her mother. Her favorite teachers, books, and school activities are alive in her interactions with her children about their schooling. Continuing this legacy, book sharing, reading together, and helping siblings with reading are accepted and expected practices. Tyreek and his brothers helped Alicia with her reading, and Alicia helped Quanzaa. Tyreek, Alicia, and Quanzaa shared an interest in the *Goosebumps* Series. Tyreek accepted his brother's social studies textbook. Leon "stole" his mother's books. Alicia got books from her brothers, mother, and neighbor. Leon loved Shakespeare. Although they did not choose to read the same texts nor were they all equally enthralled with school reading, they all valued reading. Across time, some school activities aligned with Alicia's home literacy practices and the social nature of reading in her family. When Alicia and her friends read together each morning in 1st grade or co-wrote a play in 5th grade, school practices mirrored the social literacy practices that she enjoyed at home.

These familial accounts of reading are not separate from the counter-stories (Solórzano & Yosso, 2002) related to race and schooling presented earlier. Stories about racism in schools, the need for competence with privileged forms of English, and the importance of actively challenging assumptions about poor African American families (Compton-Lilly, 2003, 2007b) contributed to the family's collective stories and the sense they made of their experiences.

In addition, race played an increasingly significant role in Alicia's reading practices. Although in 5th grade Alicia reported that race did not matter, over time the books that she reported reading and enjoying in 8th grade were increasingly connected to race. Family members valued novels written by African American authors and depicting the lives of African American people in urban communities. In 5th grade, Tyreek's biography of Martin Luther King, Alicia's biography of an African American basketball player, and her mother's interest in books by African American authors foreshadowed the importance of race in Alicia's later preferences.

Alicia and her family members often selected novels that contained counter-stories (Solórzano & Yosso, 2002) challenging dominant accounts of African American people. These stories presented the voices of African American people and were generally accounts of resistance and resilience. While some people might challenge the literary merit of the books, Alicia and her family chose stories that were realistic and relevant. They described African American people surviving difficult situations that involved economic and institutional challenges. Choosing to read books featuring African American characters in urban settings and biographies of famous African American people was not idiosyncratic. This choice reflected agency and provided participants with relevant accounts of resistance and resilience.

Historical timescales reference the historical significance of reading in African American communities and families. The Freedom Schools, biographies of Frederick Douglass, slave narratives, the histories of Black Colleges, and the writings of Marcus Garvey, W.E.B. Dubois, Langston Hughes, and Zora Neale Hurston—as well as the works of the Black authors read by Ms. Rodriguez and her children—all attest to a literate history that Alicia and her family accessed. While academic texts are part of this recorded history, television shows (i.e. *Roots, The Cosby Show*) and movies (*Amistad, Amazing Grace, Malcolm X*) also contribute to understandings of literacy in African American communities and families. As Luke (2008) reported, media representation of race and literacy contribute to the historical record; people draw upon these historic accounts as they live their lives. While Alicia and her family members may not have known the specific literacy histories of African American people and may not be able to provide dates and details related to these events and individuals, they routinely drew upon these collective histories.

Historical timescales also informed the literacy practices that Alicia encountered in school (Lemke, 2001). Traditional practices associated with English language arts classrooms contributed to the types of books Alicia was assigned to read in school. *The Baby-sitter's Club, Goosebumps*, and the African American romance novels were not among these assigned texts. None of the books that Alicia was assigned to read in school featured African American protagonists and Alicia dismissed these assigned books as boring. In addition, despite the social reading activities that Alicia shared with her 1st-grade peers and her family, school literacy had become asocial, and her reading practices no longer involved peers. Lines were drawn between literacy, peers, and Alicia's literate identity.

Alicia accessed historical timescales that referenced literacy as a dimension of her African American and school identity. She accessed familial timescales within a family that treated reading as a shared and social activity, and ongoing timescales as she described the texts she read at the time of the various interviews. Alicia's interactions across these timescales illustrate the complexity of being literate and enacting literacy. These constructions involved available resources (i.e., being African American in an urban school) and agential choices that carried their own contingencies (i.e., peer, sibling, and school expectations; see Gadsden, 2005; Lanehart, 2002). Complicated calculations of self intersected in complex ways with family, peers, schooling, and communities. They framed the reader, Alicia, in a particular time and place and in reference to other people. Across time, I witnessed Alicia's identity sedimenting and thickening. Race, peers, adolescence, and gender were part of this construction.

Identity construction involves tensions. Everyone experiences pressure from people, institutions, and social groups to behave in particular ways, and sometimes these expectations do not resonate with the values, experiences, and practices that identify people. While across time Alicia established a distance between herself and school, Alicia's reading identity was not a simple reflection of her home literacy practices. She did not share books with her friends as her mother did, or share her mother's love for English class. Unlike her mother and sister, Alicia subscribed to traditional notions of femininity (i.e., an interest in clothing, make-up), and Alicia's fixation on fulfilling feminine norms was a source of ongoing consternation for her mother and sister who both considered themselves to be tomboys.

Despite growing up in the same household, each of Alicia's siblings has a unique and recognized role in the family. As Alicia and Ms. Rodriguez explained, P.T. was interested in computers; Leon preferred music, walking, and sports; Tyreek was the artist; Alicia was the stepper; and Quanzaa was the "experience person" who enjoyed outdoor activities including sports. While these siblings have grown up in the same household, lived in the same neighborhood, and attended the same school system, they have each developed a role in the family and their own identity. These differences point to something more than simple reproduction; identity development is a complex process of incorporation and construction; family members drew upon similar resources, but in uniquely different ways.

School, home, peers, community, church, and other social groups came together across time in complex ways challenging, maintaining, and extending the ways of being, and specifically being literate, that students experienced at home. As McLeod and Yates (2006) explain, "Student subjectivities are formed in interaction with the ethos of the school, which cultivates dispositions and orientations that may contradict or correspond to the habitus formed in the family" (p. 25). Students, like Alicia, negotiate these contradictions by drawing on various resources and ways of being that they encounter across time.

CONCLUSION

An account grounded in dominant discourses could be constructed about Alicia and her family that might characterize Ms. Rodriguez as a single mother who did not graduate from high school and relied partially on welfare to support her six children. It would portray Alicia's teenage brothers as marginal students who had various encounters with the law. It might reference the gang affiliations of Alicia's friends or the fight that placed Alicia in long-term suspension in high school. I argue that these dominant discourses are dangerous constructions that draw on deficit assumptions about urban families and youth. Too often dominant discourses about families deny the histories that students bring to school, the strengths and abilities that they possess, and the critiques that they have constructed across time. Bourdieu and Passeron (1977) named this denial *symbolic violence*; Angela Valenzuela (1999) called it *subtractive schooling*. I worry that not attending to time and the ongoing, familial, and historic timescales denies possibilities for students and contributes to limited understandings on the part of teachers and researchers. As a teacher, I might have easily accepted this scenario if I had not conducted this project and come to know this family.

In this chapter, I have argued that Alicia and her family members called upon resources at historical, familial, and ongoing timescales as they defined themselves as readers and agents. By attending to timescales, researchers disrupt conventional, linear, and cumulative notions of time, demonstrating that students and family members access time in recursive and future-oriented ways as they engage in identity construction. The temporal experiences of students, like Alicia, can help educators recognize the ways family histories and the stories that are told and retold within families relate to larger social histories and resonate with and against students' educational experiences. By attending to time, researchers and educators can begin to recognize students as agents who draw on the resources that are available to them at multiple timescales to make sense of their world and their role in that world as they construct their identities as students and as readers.

Conclusion: Reading Time

Ms. Webster: We had to fight just to learn to read.
Ms. Holt: [Reading was] not that enjoyable.
   They were trying to make me read.
Mr. Sherwood: They just give you the book
   [pause], and you supposed to read it.
Ms. Webster: [Some teachers were] stuck on the work.

Powerful phrases like these highlight the ways that parents made sense of experiences related to reading and schooling across time. Throughout the project, parents recounted memories and told stories about school, their parents, and their children. I witnessed families change, children grow up, and unanticipated events occur. Discourses recurred in multiple interviews, artifacts brought historical meanings to classrooms, and cultural models determined the ways parents and children interpreted their worlds. In this longitudinal research project, time became visible in ways I could not have imagined. Time was the context in which people operated, a tool they used to make sense of their worlds, and a resource that was allocated in schools.

FIVE TEMPORAL PREMISES

Based on the multilayered relevance of time in this study, I maintain that it would behoove qualitative researchers to attend explicitly to time, especially when they address issues that involve long-term processes such as identity construction, school achievement, and literacy learning. To demonstrate the relevance of time, I return to the five temporal premises that were presented in the Introduction and developed further in Chapter 1.

People's Understandings of the World Are Constructed, Refined, Revised, and Abandoned over Time

Throughout this study, the words of my former students and their parents suggest that people draw upon multiple timescales to make sense of their worlds. Parents reflected on their own school experiences as they made sense of their children's progress in school. They described favorite teachers and applied these insights to the accounts of their children's teachers. Children's assessments of books and other texts changed over time and involved distinctions between series books, schoolbooks, magazines, and books that had been made into movies. Simultaneously, reasons for reading and discourses about being a good reader were constructed and deconstructed. Being a good reader was sometimes connected to being promoted to the next grade level or graduating high school; at other times it involved home reading practices that were neither recognized nor valued in school.

Now and then discourses related to how kids are taught to read, the potential role of technology in schools, and the different and increasingly complex world that kids must navigate were voiced in the instructional stories that parents told their children. In these examples, the past was called upon to serve the interests of participants in the present and inform potential futures. Children's occupational aspirations drew upon long established cultural models that designated boy jobs and girl jobs. Similarly, parental faith in children was grounded in longitudinal knowledge of students; while stories were revised over time, faith endured. In all cases, it was clear that understandings of the world were embedded in time and the historical and familial timescales in which people operated.

Understandings of Self Are Constructed over Time as People Draw upon Past Experiences and Envision Future Possibilities

Not only were meanings about the world constructed over time, but participants also constructed understandings about themselves. Student and parents enacted identities through the books they read and those they did not. Choosing magazines focused on current events over historical texts spoke to the interests and concerns of youth. David's claim to enjoy the books he was assigned to read meant something—David positioned himself as a serious student. Keeping up with instruction and assignments at school was evidence of being smart. Favorite teachers of the past informed the present as parents encountered their children's teachers and as children draw on familial lessons to describe their teachers.

In some cases, students negotiated their identities during the interviews. Christy questioned me about her mother, and Javon wondered if he was chosen for the interviews because he was "busy in class." Finally, historical timescales were evoked as accounts of racial segregation and limited opportunities in the past converged with critiques of current special education policies. Parents were distinctly aware of historically-based assumptions related to their use of African American Language, attending urban schools, and living in a ghetto community.

Institutional Time Is Related to Teaching and Learning

Schools are institutions that generally involve expectations related to covering material and the pace of instruction. Students described their teachers as providing time, making time, taking time, and giving time. They complained about teachers who taught too fast, did not help students review for tests, and conducted long boring classes. Javon gave up on reading Harry Potter in order to meet his 25-book goal for the year. These instructional dimensions occurred alongside school policies related to time that included hall checks at passing time, daily schedules, semesters, and marking periods. As Ms. Webster lamented when the children were in grade 1, some teachers were "stuck on the work" rather than attending to their students. Despite their critiques of schooling, parents and students displayed remarkable faith that schools will provide their children with the experiences they will access to meet their goals.

People Are Temporal Beings Who Are Caught Up Within Multiple Dimensions of Time

Shared social histories, personal pasts, and ongoing experiences operated together as parents and students negotiated schooling and literacy learning. The stories that parents told of their children, the stories teachers told to their students, and the histories of local communities intertwined. Personal, familial, and historic pasts were all connected. Race, gender, and social class mattered in terms of the vocations students chose and the books they read. Knowing children over time meant that accomplishments and enactments of the past were part of who they were understood to be in the present and would become in the future. In several cases, the voices of people who had passed away years ago continued to be recounted.

Schools and Research Initiatives Bring Their Own Particular Temporal Expectations and Practices

School systems and educational research projects are generally organized to deal with groups of students for relatively short periods of time. Traditional approaches to schooling focus on children over short periods of time (e.g., school years, semesters, marking periods), while researchers tend to rely on short-term funding sources and the demands of tenure and academia. However, there have been a few notable examples of longitudinal qualitative work in education. Comber and Barnett (2003) followed 20 children for 5 years through elementary school. They reported on the children's literacy learning and noted how with support from teachers and parents some children who had fallen behind were able to catch up to their peers. In a study that followed 26 middle school students for 6 years—through the end of high school—McLeod and Yates (2006) examined vocational aspirations and the ways students conceptualized being a good student across the 6-year study. Suárez-Orozco, Suárez-Orozco, and Todorova (2008) designed a mixed method study that included qualitative interviews, narrative construction tasks, and ethnographic methods to create 75 case portraitures of immigrant students over a 5-year period to explore the issues and challenges faced by immigrant families. Finally, a few prominent qualitative researchers in the field of education, including Luis Moll (Gonzalez, Moll, & Amanti, 2005; Moll, Amanti, Neff,& Gonzalez, 1992) and Elizabeth Moje, (Moje, Ciechanowski, Kramer, Ellis, Carrillo, & Collazo, 2004; Moje, Overby, Tysvaer, & Morris, 2008), are in the process of conducting longitudinal projects that promise to contribute to this growing body of knowledge about children and communities across time.

This work is paving the way for new thinking about students and the long-term processes that they engage with as they move through school. As educators and researchers focus on students as living within time, they can begin to envision children as people who draw on lived pasts grounded in families and larger social histories. I present this example of long-term longitudinal research as an example of what can be learned and suggest that longitudinal research has the potential to significantly impact our understandings about literacy learning, schooling, and identity construction.

THE POTENTIAL OF LONGITUDINAL QUALITATIVE RESEARCH AND TIME

Longitudinal qualitative research allows researchers to view students and families as more than static and easily-identified stereotypical sorts of people. The young man who enters a high school classroom wearing a baggy shirt and drooping blue jeans is not only what he appears to be today. He brings a bricolage of experiences and insights. He is making sense of his experiences, while gathering stories and counter-stories that reflect his experiences as well as the experiences of his family, peers, and classmates.

While teachers cannot travel back in time to visit their students at earlier ages, they can recognize students as temporal beings who bring experiences and knowledge to classrooms. I encourage educators and researchers to consider time in order to gain more nuanced understandings of their students. I maintain that there are three critical considerations. First, it is essential that educators and researchers listen to the stories and counter-stories told by children and their family members. These stories are grounded in historic realities that affect the meanings people make of the present and their plans for the future. Part of this means demonstrating respect for the critiques that students and their family members bring to school and recognizing these critiques as genuine, valid, and essential knowledge for students who must learn to navigate complex social contexts in school and beyond.

Second, educators and researchers must attend to the types of literacy experiences offered to students. It is essential that educators provide experiences and texts that are compatible with students' evolving identities. Educators and researchers cannot ask students to buy into literacy unless the literacy experiences have relevance and entail activities that students can envision themselves enacting. This requires that educators learn about literate practices that students might be hesitant to share in classrooms. At the same time, it means assisting students in finding ways to expand their existing range of literacy practices—inviting students to fall in love with new types of texts and literate experiences and/or recognizing the ways students can use a range of literacy practices to achieve their goals. Not all texts need to focus on minority youth, adolescent issues, or challenges related to social class; however, there must be something in every text that is compatible with students' views of themselves and teachers must help students to make these connections.

Student identities relative to literacy and schooling are multifaceted, flexible, and evolving. There is always the potential for growth when educators and researchers focus on students' capacities to take on new interests and identities. In addition, we must always remember that teachers and researchers access ongoing experiences, as well as familial and historical resources as we continuously construct ourselves as readers and as people. Working with students from diverse backgrounds requires teachers and educators to step away from their own experiences and histories to consider other ways of knowing the world.

I agree with Leander (2001), who says "The management of space-time in pedagogy may be a means of bracketing and constraining particular identities while privileging others" (p. 673). Experiences in school across time, over generations, and in negotiation with past accounts and future dreams offer students and their families variously possible literate identities. What people read is not just about the books they like, but also about the literate identities they enact or reject. Enjoying school-assigned texts has consequences—good and bad. Low-income families are not composed of people who fail to provide kids with assumedly essential literacy experiences; they are spaces where families grapple at the intersection of multiple literacy practices, the meanings of these experiences, and the affiliations that accompany literate practices.

There are certainly limitations to the present study and additional studies are needed. First, the current study focused on children and their parents; little attention was paid to the perspectives of teachers and no attention was paid to the voices of administrators, policy makers, and community members. This study did not access cumulative school records that contain significant longitudinal accounts. In addition, there are numerous gaps in the data; significant events may have occurred during years when I was not collecting data, specifically during grades 2, 3, 4, 6, and 7. Finally, we do not have a clear understanding of how time operates in identity construction for children from diverse communities, including privileged, upper class families. It is very possible that counter-stories circulate in some of these homes as well and contribute to identity construction in these families.

Despite these limits, this research project provides a useful example of the potential of long-term longitudinal research to complicate and inform the ways researchers and educators understand issues related to literacy, literate identity, and schooling. Teachers play a role in recognizing students as people who bring particular histories to their classrooms. Teachers access a variety of historic, familial, and ongoing timescales. They can tap historic timescales that identify African American students as people who bring rich literate histories to classrooms. Educators can treat their students as people whose lived experiences have provided them with deep critical and significant analyses of schooling and society. Researchers can learn about students' everyday literate practices and interests—countering majoritarian accounts that deny the histories they and their families bring and focus on what is viewed as missing or problematic in relation to test scores, behaviors, current academic standards, and grade level expectations. Attention to timescales enables educators to attend to what students bring—not just in terms of what they can do but in terms of what they have lived, the social relations that have contributed to their ways of being, and the larger histories that they access. As Lemke (2005) maintained, "We construct meaning of our lives . . . across multiple timescales of action and activity, from the blink of an eye to the work of a lifetime" (p. 110). Our challenge as educators is to recognize and work with the vast stores of experiences and knowledge that children bring and part of that involves attending to understandings and meanings as constructed across time.

Family Overviews

Parent/Child	Gender	Age	Employment	Education	Family	Ethnicity
Ms. Burns	F		grocery store	Associate's degree	married	European American
Angela	F	13				European American
Ms. Hernandez*	F	30	dry cleaner	Not graduated	single	Puerto Rican
Jasmine	F	13				Puerto Rican
Ms. Holt	F	50	disability	Graduated high school	single	African American
Bradford	M	14				African American
Ms. Horner	F	32	unemployed	GED	separated	European American
Peter	M	13				European American
Ms. Hudson	F	48	disabilty	Not graduated	married	African American
Jermaine	M	13		home/health certificate		African American
Ms. Johnson	F	41	food service	GED, business school	widowed	European American
David	M	13				Biracial
Ms. Mason	F	43	preschool teacher	Graduated high school	single	African American

Parent/Child	Gender	Age	Employment	Education	Family	Ethnicity
Javon	M	13				African American
Ms. Rodriguez	F	40	day care	GED, child care certificate	single	African American
Alicia	F	13				African American
Ms. Denver* (adopted mother)	F		day care	Not graduated	married	African American
Ms. Robins* (foster mother)	F		day care	Not graduated	married	African American
Ms. Green-Abdul	F	47	unemployed	Associate's degree	widowed	European American
Christy	F	14				Biracial
Mr. Sherwood*	M	55	maintenance	Graduated high school	married	African American
Marvin	M	14		trade school		African American
Ms. Webster*	F	35	secretarial	Graduated high school	single	European American
Tiffany	F	13		computer/job training classes		Biracial

*Mr. Sherwood is Marvin's step-grandfather; he and Marvin's grandmother have primary responsibility for Marvin; Ms. Denver is Christy's adoptive-mother; she has legal guardianship of Christy; Ms. Robins was Christy's foster-mother; she had legal guardianship of Christy; Ms. Hernandez and Ms. Webster participated in earlier phases of the study.

A Longitudinal Qualitative Research Project: Methodology

In his book on longitudinal qualitative research, Saldaña (2003) did not specify a time requirement for such research, stating only that "longitudinal research means a *lonnnnnnng* time" (p. 1). In his view, longitudinal research helps researchers:

1. view the breadth and depth of people's life experiences, and
2. document change by comparing data collected through long-term observations of actors and their perspectives.

My longitudinal project allowed me to collect data during long-term processes of literacy learning, schooling, and identity construction. From grades 1 through 8, I visited with families at 3- and 4-year intervals. The "periodic restudy" (Saldaña, 2003) of the same families at 3- and 4-year intervals enabled me to follow the families for a significant period of time without becoming overly intrusive in their lives. In addition, by limiting my visits I limited the amount of data collected and avoided producing unmanageable amounts of data. In addition to the three phases described in this book, I have returned to visit the families when the students were in high school and continue to analyze these data.

My goal has always been to gain an understanding, although inevitably and admittedly incomplete and filtered through my own experiences, of the meanings that students and their parents bring to literacy. The data I offer in this book does not represent truth; it represents my understandings of people's interpretations and presentations of themselves and their experiences over time. Garfinkel (1967) invited researchers to treat our everyday experiences, circumstances, and understandings of our worlds as the subjects of contemplation; few things are more everyday and unavoidable than time. Yet it is critical to recognize that the uniqueness of participants' understandings does not reduce their experiences to personal accounts. The people described in this book shared a history. Not only were the children members of the same 1st-grade class, lived in the same low-income community, and attended schools in the same district, but, with the exception of Angela, who as described below was added to the sample when she was in 5th grade to replace a child who had moved, they also shared social positionings related to race and social class.

THE RESEARCH SETTING AND PARTICIPANTS

During the initial phase, I asked the parents of ten randomly selected students from my 1st-grade class, along with their children, to participate in a series of interviews that focused on concepts about reading. Eventually, the families participated during the children's 1st-grade year, 4th/5th-grade year, and 7th/8th-grade year.

In 1st grade, the original students attended Rosa Parks Elementary School; 97% of the students in that school qualified for free or reduced-priced lunch. The city in which the school was located continues to struggle with unemployment, substandard housing, a lack of quality physical and mental health care, the closing of local libraries, gang violence, and a proliferation of illegal businesses, including drug trafficking. Despite these depressing descriptors, most of the families in the community were committed to their children and active in ensuring that their children did well in school. By middle school, eight students from the original sample remained in the project and attended schools across the district; two had moved out of the school district and could not be located.

When I went back to locate families when the children were in 4th or 5th grade, I was unable to locate Tiffany. By that time, I was confident that I would be following the students into high school, and I was concerned about losing families from the sample over time. Thus, I created a plan to strategically replace students in the sample. Angela was a 5th grader who had a younger sister who at the time I added Angela to the sample was in my 1st-grade classroom. The child who had left the sample was biracial (European American and Arabic American), Angela was European American and the closest demographic match. Both Angela and her younger sister, Meg, participated in interviews. When the students were in grades seven and eight, I was able to locate eight of the original ten students. Jasmine and her mother had left the school district and could not be located for the middle school interviews. By that time, I was confident that I would have sufficient students to complete the project, and I made the decision not to replace other students. Although Jasmine and Tiffany left the sample prior to middle school, in some places in this book, I include data from earlier phases as their voices contribute to the issues being discussed.

DATA COLLECTION

Throughout the project multiple data sources were collected to capture the complexity and the situated nature of students' experiences. Interviews were critical as they captured perspectives of students and their parents relative to reading, schooling, and self.

While the initial phase included a range of data sources including parent and student interviews, fieldnotes, portfolio and classroom assessments, and audiotapes of classroom discussions (see Figure B.1), during phases two and three I collected parent and child interviews, reading assessments, writing samples, and standardized test scores. Interviews with parents lasted approximately sixty minutes; early interviews with children were shorter, lasting approximately twenty minutes—as the children grew older their interviews grew longer. By the time students were in middle school their interviews lasted approximately an hour.

In elementary school, I asked the children about their experiences at home and school with reading and writing, experiences with learning to read, book preferences, experiences with computers, and plans for the future. In middle school, I also asked them about their favorite classes, teachers, friends, and interests outside of school. I asked their parents about their own childhood experiences with learning to read, school experiences, reading and writing practices, opinions about literacy and technology, satisfaction with their children's school experiences, their hopes for their children's futures, the literacy experiences they shared with their children, and themselves as readers. With the exception of the 1st-grade interviews with children that occurred at school and some fifth grade interviews that were conducted at local fast food restaurants, all other interviews occurred in homes; interviews were audiotaped and detailed written notes were recorded.

DATA ANALYSIS

Analyzing data from this longitudinal project involved managing a large data set collected over eight years. The process involved three separate and lengthy processes of transcription, coding, and analysis. The same general procedure was used during each phase. Either myself, or a professional transcriptionist, transcribed the interview audiotapes. Then, I personally checked and edited the transcriptions. Data analysis programs, first Hyperqual and later Nvivo, were used to sort segments of interviews into code sets that were suggested by multiple readings of the transcripts. The initial code sets were supplemented, expanded, condensed, combined, and abandoned as more and more interviews were coded and as other data sources were

Figure B.1: Research Phases, Participants, Data and Analysis

Phase	Participants	Data	Analysis
Grade 1	10 families	4 Parent interviews 4 Student interviews Fieldnotes Portfolio/classroom assessments Classroom discussions	Coding across studies
Grades 4/5	9 original families 1 new family	2 Parent interviews 2 Student interviews Reading assessments Writing samples	Case study development
Grades 7/8	8 original families 1 family added in grades 4/5	2 Parent interviews 2 Student interviews Reading assessments Writing samples	Coding across studies
Grades 8–11	7 original families 1 family added in grades 4/5	3 Parent interviews 3 Student interviews Reading assessments Writing samples School observations Teacher interviews Student-created writing, photos, audiotapes journals, and/or drawings	Case study development

added to the evolving data set. At times, transcripts that were coded early in the analysis process were revisited during later stages to reflect the revised code book. Once all interviews were coded, I conducted a close reading of each code set and again revised, condensed, and combined existing code sets as needed. For example, I combined code sets that were similar or re-sorted data from particularly large code sets to reflect more specific issues. Finally, I clustered the code sets around shared themes as I identified larger themes related to my research interests.

Data coding for each phase of the project followed the general process described above with one difference; during phases one and three, I coded data across the entire data set. During the second phase, I coded the data from each family separately and constructed case summaries for each family prior to identifying inter-case patterns. This process of moving between general analytical categories and case study analyses has supported a balance between identifying themes shared across cases and maintaining attention to unique and individual dimensions of each case.

As I coded data from phase three, codes related to time emerged. Close analysis of the data, alongside my long-term relationships with the families, revealed time as a constitutive dimension of experience that people used to conceptualize literacy, schooling, and themselves. In middle school, three of the students were a year behind in school and Jermaine was two years behind. In addition to falling behind chronologically, several students and parents complained about the fast pace of instruction, discussed the achievement expectations that accompanied schooling, worried about the coverage of material in special education classrooms, and spoke about students' reading levels and abilities relative to their grade levels. Furthermore, discourse analysis of interview data from phase three resulted in a set of codes related to time ("time," "change," "future," "now and then"). Specifically, I noted and coded participants' explicit use of temporal language (e.g., "now," "then," "someday," "next week," "after," "fast"). Finally, I noted how participants recursively and selectively drew on experiences across time as they repeatedly returned to some stories while neglecting and forgetting others or framed some stories as examples of larger patterns. Some books and literacy practices were mentioned at multiple interviews; others were forgotten. In some instances, participants voiced and re-voiced the same comments using almost the same words across long periods of time.

Significantly, my recognition of time required me to reread and re-analyze the data from the various phases to attend to patterns across these phases. I reread the data seeking repeated stories, references to time, and repeated discourses. It is critical to recognize that focusing on events and patterns at particular points in time can actually obfuscate longitudinal patterns. Thus, it is essential for longitudinal qualitative researchers to be attentive to long-term patterns that may not be apparent with traditional analytical processes.

To a great degree, the methods used in this project have been created and refined as I moved through the process. However, these procedures also draw upon well-established methods in the field including ethno-graphic approaches, discourse analysis, and case study methods. As Neale and Flowerdale (2003) report, most projects resemble snapshots rather than movies; they capture points in time rather than ongoing actions and interactions. While no project, including the one described in this book, could capture a person's every interaction and experience, the current project has captured multiple snapshots across a long period of time. In addition, participants have often recounted or commented on events that occurred between phases allowing me to consider the ways my students and their families made sense of their lives over time.

References

Adam, B. (1990). *Time and social theory*. Cambridge, UK: Polity Press.
Adam, B. (2008). The timescapes challenge: Engagement with the invisible temporal. In R. Edwards (Ed.), *Researching lives through time: Time, generation, and life stories* [Timescapes working paper series no. 1]. Leeds, UK: University of Leeds. Available at http://www.timescapes.leeds.ac.uk/events-dissemination/publications.php
Allington, R. (2000). *What really matters for struggling readers: Designing research based-programs*. New York: Allyn and Bacon.
Auerbach, E. (1989). Toward a socio-contextual approach to family literacy. *Harvard Educational Review, 59(2)*, 165–187.
Bakhtin, M. M. (1981). *The dialogic imagination: Four essays by M. M. Bakhtin*. (C. Emerson & M. Holquist Trans.). Austin: University of Texas Press.
Bakhtin, M. M. (1994). From M. M. Bakhtin, the dialogic imagination. In P. Morris (Ed.), *The Bakhtin reader: Selected writings of Bakhtin, Medvedev, Voloshinov* (pp. 74–80). London: Edward Arnold.
Bandura, A., Barbaranelli, C., Campara, G. V., & Pastorelli, C. (2001). Self-efficacy beliefs as shapers of children's aspirations and career trajectories. *Child Development, 71(1)*, 187–206.
Bourdieu, P., & Passeron, J. (1977). *Reproduction in education, society, and culture*. London: Sage.
Callahan, R. E. (1962). *Education and the cult of efficiency*. Chicago: University of Chicago Press.
Clay, M. M. (2001). *Change over time in children's literacy development*. Portsmouth, NH: Heinemann.
Clay, M. M. (2005). *Literacy lessons: Designed for individuals* (Vols. 1 & 2). Portsmouth, NH: Heinemann.
Comber, B., & Barnett, J. (2003). *Look again: Longitudinal studies of children's literacy learning*. New South Wales, Australia: Primary English Teaching Association.
Comber, B., Badger, L., Barnett, J., Nixon, H., & Pitt, J. (2002). *Literacy after the early years: A longitudinal study*. Retrieved from www.myread.org on 9/30/11.
Compton-Lilly, C. (2003). *Reading families: The literate lives of urban children*. New York: Teachers College Press.
Compton-Lilly, C. (2005). "Sounding out": A pervasive cultural model of reading. *Language Arts, 82(6)*, 441–451.

Compton-Lilly, C. (2007a). Exploring reading capital in two Puerto Rican families. *Reading Research Quarterly, 42*(1), 72–98.

Compton-Lilly, C. (2007b). *Rereading families: The literate lives of urban children, four years later*. New York: Teachers College Press.

Cremin, L. (1990). *American education: The metropolitan experience, 1876–1980*. New York: HarperCollins.

Dalbert, C. (2004). The implications and functions of just and unjust experiences in school. In C. Dalbert & H. Sallay (Eds.), *The justice motive in adolescence and young adulthood: Origins and consequences* (pp. 117–134). New York: Routledge.

Davila, D., & Patrick, L. (2010). Asking the experts: What children have to say about their reading preferences. *Language Arts, 87*(3), 199–210.

Dyson, A. H. (2003). *The brothers and sisters learn to write*. New York: Teachers College Press.

Elkind, D. (1971). Teacher-child contracts. *The School Review, 79*(4), 579–589.

Emig, J. (1977). Writing as a mode of learning. *College Composition and Communication, 28*(2), pp. 122–128.

Enciso, P. (2007). Reframing history in sociocultural theory: Toward an expansive vision. In Lewis, C., Enciso, P., & Moje, E. B. (Eds.), *Reframing sociocultural research on literacy: Identity, agency, and power* (pp. 49–74). Mahwah, NJ: Lawrence Erlbaum.

Feitelson, D., Kita, B., & Goldstein, Z. (1986). Effects of listening to series stories on first graders' comprehension and use of language. *Research in the Teaching of English, 20*(4), 339–356.

Feldlaufer, H., Midgley, C., & Eccles, J. S. (1988). Student, teachers, and observer perceptions of the classroom environment before and after the transition to junior high school. *Journal of Early Adolescence, 8*(2), pp. 133–156.

Gabriel, R., & Allington, R. (2009). Middle schools and magazines: Can they read difficult but self-selected materials? Presentation for the National Reading Conference. December 2009, Albuquerque, NM.

Gadsden, V. (2000). Intergenerational literacy within families. In P. D. Pearson, R. Barr, M. Kamil, & P. Mosenthal (Eds.), *Handbook of reading research* (pp. 871–887). New York: Longman.

Gadsden, V. (2005). Intergenerational discourses: Life texts of African-American mothers and daughters. In J. Flood, S. B. Heath, & D. Lapp (Eds.), *Handbook of research on teaching literacy through the communicative and visual arts* (pp. 376–385). Mahwah, NJ: Lawrence Erlbaum.

Garfinkel, H. (1967). *Studies in ethnomethodology*. Englewood Cliffs, NJ: Prentice-Hall.

Gee, J. P. (1990). *Social linguistics and literacies: Ideologies in discourses*. London: Falmer Press.

Gee, J. (1999). *An introduction to discourse analysis: Theory and method*. New York: Routledge.

Genishi, C., & Dyson, A. H. (2009). *Children, language, and literacy*. New York: Teachers College Press.

Gergen, K. J. (1984). An introduction to historical social psychology. In K. J. Gergen & M. M. Gergen (Eds.), *Historical social psychology* (pp. 3–36). Hillsdale, NJ: Erlbaum.

Gonzalez, N., Moll, L. C., & Amanti, C. (2005). *Funds of knowledge: Theorizing practices in households, communities, and classrooms.* New York: Teachers College Press.

Gottfredson, L. S., & Becker, H. J. (1981). A challenge to vocational psychology: How important are aspirations in determining male career development. *Journal of Vocational Behavior, 18*(2), 121–137.

Graff, H. (1979). *The literacy myth: Literacy and social structure in the nineteenth-century city.* New York: Academic Press.

Graff, J. M. (2010). Reading, readin' and skimming: Preadolescent girls navigate the sociocultural landscapes of books and reading. *Language Arts, 87*(3), 177–187.

Greenlee, A. A., Monson, D. L., & Taylor, B. M. (1996). The lure of series books: Does it affect the appreciation for recommended literature? *The Reading Teacher, 50*(3), 216–225.

Gutiérrez, K. (2007). Commentary on part I: Rethinking conceptual frameworks. In C. Lewis, P. Enciso, & E. B. Moje (Eds.), *Reframing sociocultural research and literacy: Identity, agency, and power* (pp. 115–120). Mahwah, NJ: Lawrence Erlbaum.

Hall, C., & Coles, M. (1999). Children's reading choices. New York: Routledge.

Hartung, P. J., Porfeli, E. J., & Vondracek, F. W. (2004). Child vocational development: A review and reconsideration. *Journal of Vocational Behavior, 66*(3), 385–419.

Heath, S. B. (1983). *Ways with words: Language, life and work in communities and classrooms.* New York: Cambridge University Press.

Heath, S. B. (2001). The children of Trackton's children: Spoken and written language in social change. In E. Cushman, B. Kintgen, B. Kroll, & M. Rose (Eds.), *Literacy: A critical sourcebook* (pp. 156–172). New York: St. Martin's Press.

Heidegger, M. (1962). *Being and time.* San Francisco: Harper and Row.

Ivey, G., & Broaddus, K. (2001). "Just plain reading": A survey of what makes students want to read in middle school classrooms. *Reading Research Quarterly, 36*(4), 350–377.

Jacobs, G. (2009). A simplified timeline of media practices. Presentation at 12th Annual Xerox Center Conference, Xerox Multicultural Center at SUNY Geneseo, Geneseo, New York.

Jencks, C., & Phillips, M., Eds. (1998). *The Black-White test score gap.* Washington, DC: Brookings Institution Press.

Kimmel, E. (1982). Children's literature without children. *Children's Literature in Education, 13*(1), pp. 38–43.

Kozol, J. (1991). *Savage inequalities: Children in America's schools.* New York: Crown Publishers.

Krashen, S. (1993). *The power of reading.* Englewood, CO: Libraries Unlimited.

Kriedberg, G., Butcher, A. L., & White, K. M. (1978). Vocational role choice in second- and sixth-grade children. *Sex Roles, 4*(2), 175–181.

Laccour, P. (1980). Narrative time. *Critical Inquiry, 7*(1), 169–190.

Ladson-Billings, G. (1994). *The dreamkeepers: Successful teachers of African American children.* San Francisco: Jossey-Bass.

Ladson-Billings, G. (2009). "Why can't we read something good?" How "standards," "testing," and scripted curricula impoverish urban students. National Reading Conference. December 2009, Albuquerque, NM.

Ladson-Billings, G., & Tate, W. (1995). Toward a critical race theory of education. *Teachers College Record, 97* (1), 47–68.

Lanehart, S. (2002). *Sista, Speak! Black women kinfolk talk about language and literacy.* Austin, TX: University of Texas Press.

Lareau, A. (2003). *Unequal childhoods: Class, race, and family life.* Berkeley: University of California Press.

Leander, K. (2001). "This is our freedom bus going home right now": Producing and hybridizing space-time contexts in pedagogical discourse. *Journal of Literacy Research, 33*(4), 637–679.

Lee, C. D. (2007). *Culture, literacy, and learning: Taking bloom in the midst of the whirlwind.* New York: Teachers College Press.

Lemke, J. (1995). *Textual politics: Discourse and social dynamics.* New York: Taylor and Francis.

Lemke, J. (2000). Across the scales of time: Artifacts, activities, and meanings in ecosocial systems. *Mind, Culture, and Activity, 7*(4), 273–290.

Lemke, J. (2001). The long and short of it: Comments on multiple timescale studies of human activity. *The Journal of the Learning Sciences, 10*(1&2), 17–26.

Lemke, J. (2005). Place, pace and meaning: Multimedia chronotopes. In S. Norris & R. Jones (Eds.), *Discourse in action: Introducing mediated discourse analysis* (pp. 110–122). New York: Routledge.

Levine, R. (1997). *A geography of time: The temporal misadventures of a social psychologist.* New York: Basic Books.

Looft, W. R. (1971). Sex differences in the expression of vocational aspirations by elementary children. *Developmental Psychology, 5*(2), 366.

Luke, A. (1987). Making Dick and Jane: Historical genesis of the modern basal reader. *Teachers College Record, 89*(1), 91–116.

Luke, A. (2008). Another ethnic autobiography? Childhood and the cultural economy of looking. In R. Hammer, & D. Kellner (Eds.), *Media/Cultural studies* (pp. 482–500). New York: Peter Lang.

Mackey, M. (1990). Filling the gaps: The baby-sitter's club and the learning reader. *Language Arts, 67*(5), 484–489.

McLeod, J., & Yates, L. (2006). *Making modern lives: Subjectivity, schooling, and social change.* Albany, NY: State University Press.

McLeod, J., & Thomson, R. (2009). *Researching social change: Qualitative approaches.* Los Angeles: Sage Publications.

Metcalfe, A., & Game, A. (2007). Becoming who you are: The time of education. *Time and Society, 16*(1), 43–59.

Miller, D. (2010). Becoming a classroom of readers. *Educational Researcher, 67*(6), 30–35.

Moje, E. B., Overby, M., Tysvaer, N., & Morris, K. (2008). The complex world of adolescent literacy: Myths, motivations, and mysteries. *Harvard Educational Review*, 107–154.

Moje, E. B., Ciechanowski, K., Kramer, K., Ellis, L., Carrillo, R., & Collazo, T. (2004). Working toward third space in content area literacy: An examination of everyday funds of knowledge and discourse. *Reading Research Quarterly, 39*(1), 38–71.

Moll, L. C., Amanti, C., Neff, D., & Gonzalez, N. (1992). Funds of knowledge for teaching: Using a qualitative approach to connect homes and classrooms. *Theory into Practice, 31*(1), 132–141.

Neale, B., & Flowerdale, J. (2003). Time, texture, and childhood: The contours of longitudinal qualitative research. *International Journal of Social Research Methodology, 6*(3), 189–199.

O'Keefe, E. S., & Hyde, J. S. (1983). The development of occupational sex-role stereotypes: The effects of gender stability and age. *Sex Roles, 9*(4), 481–492.

Pahl, K. (2007) Timescales and ethnography: Understanding a child's meaning-making across three sites, a home, a classroom and a family literacy class. *Ethnography and Education, 2*(2), 175–190.

Pettigrew, A. M. (1995). Longitudinal field research on change: Theory and practice. In G. P. Huber & A. H. Van de Van (Eds.), *Longitudinal field research methods* (pp. 91–125). Thousand Oaks, CA: Sage.

Reese, L., Kroesen, K., & Gallimore, R. (2000). Agency and school performance among urban Latino youth. In R. D. Taylor & M. C. Wang (Eds.), *Resilience across contexts: Family, work, culture and community* (pp. 295–332). Mahwah, NJ: Lawrence Erlbaum.

Reid, L., & Cline, R. (1997). Our repressed reading addictions: Teachers and young adult series books. *The English Journal, 86*(3), 68–72.

Rist, R. (1978). *The invisible children: School integration in American society.* Cambridge, MA: Harvard University Press.

Rogers, R. (2003). *A critical discourse analysis of family literacy practices: Power in and out of school.* Mahwah, NJ: Lawrence Erlbaum.

Rosen, B. C. (1959). Ethnicity and the achievement syndrome. *American Sociological Review, 24*(1), 47–60.

Rosenblatt, L. (1994). *The reader, the text, and the poem: The transactional theory of the literary work.* Carbondale, IL: Southern Illinois University Press.

Ross, C. S. (1995). "If they read Nancy Drew, so what?" Series book readers talk back. *Library Information and Science Research, 17*(3), 201–236.

Saldaña, J. (2003). *Longitudinal research: Analyzing change through time.* Walnut Creek, CA: Altamira Press.

Saltman, J. (1997). Groaning under the weight of series books. *Emergency Librarian, 24*(5), 23–25.

Schulenberg, J. E., Vondracek, F. W., & Crouter, A. C. (1984). The influence of family on vocational development. *Journal of Marriage and the Family, 46*(1), 129–143.

Sewell, W. H., Haller, A. O., & Strauss, M. A. (1957). Social status and educational and occupational aspiration. *American Sociological Review, 22*(1), 67–73.

Smith, F. (1987). *Joining the literacy club.* Portsmouth, NH: Heinemann.

Smitherman, G. (2006). *Word from the mother: Language and African Americans.* New York: Routledge.

Solórzano, D. G., & Yosso, T. J. (2002). Critical race methodology: Counter-storytelling as an analytical framework for educational research. *Qualitative Inquiry, 8*(1), 23–44.

Spencer, M. B., & Markstrom-Adams, C. (1990). Identity processes among racial and minority children in America. *Child Development, 61*(2), 290–310.

Strommen, L. T., & Mates, B. F. (2004). Learning to love reading: Interviews with older children and teens. *Journal of Adolescent and Adult Literacy, 48*(3), 188–200.

Suárez-Orozco, C., Suárez-Orozco, M., & Todorova, I. (2008). *Learning in a new land: Immigrant students in American society.* Cambridge, MA: Harvard University Press.

Taylor, D. (1983). *Family literacy: Young children learning to read and write.* Portsmouth, NH: Heinemann.

Toppo, G. (2004, February 25). See 'Dick and Jane'—again. *USA Today.* Viewed at http://www.usatoday.com/life/books/news/2004-02-25-dick-and-jane-main_x.htm

Trice, A. D. (1991). Stability of children's career aspirations. *Journal of Genetic Psychology, 152*(1), 137–139.

Ujiie, J., & Krashen, S. (2002). Home run books and reading enjoyment. *Knowledge Quest, 31*(3), 36–37.

Valenzuela, A. (1999). *Subtractive schooling: U.S.-Mexican youth and the politics of caring.* Albany, New York: State University of New York Press.

Watson, M., & McMahon, M. (2005). Children's career development: A research review from a learning perspective. *Journal of Vocational Behavior, 67*(2), 119–132.

Wortham, S. (2006). *Learning identity: The joint emergence of social identification and academic learning.* Cambridge, UK: Cambridge University Press.

Worthy, J. (1996). A matter of interest: Literature that hooks reluctant readers and keeps them reading. *The Reading Teacher, 50*(3), 204–212.

Worthy, J., Moorman, M., & Turner, M. (1999). What Johnny likes to read is hard to find in school. *Reading Research Quarterly, 34*(1), 12–27.

LITERATURE REFERENCES

Bridwell, N. (1963–current). *Clifford the big red dog* series. New York: Scholastic.

Brown, M. (1982–current). *Arthur* Series. New York: Scholastic.

Davidson, M. (1989). *Frederick Douglass fights for freedom.* New York: Scholastic Publishing.

Dixon, F. W. (1927–current). *The Hardy boys* series. Grosset & Dunlap.

Faulkner, W. (1931/2007). *A rose for Emily.* New York: Perfection Learning.

Forester, C. S. (1951). *Lieutenant Hornblower.* New York: Back Bay Books.

George, J. (1988). *Cry of the crow.* New York: HarperCollins.

George, J. (1997). *There's an owl in the shower.* New York: HarperTrophy.

Goines, D. (1973). *White man's justice, black man's grief.* New York: Holloway House.

Guy, R. (1991). *Ruby.* East Orange, NJ: Just Us Books.

Hansberry, L. (1958/2002). *A raisin in the sun.* New York: Random House.

Henke, K. (2005). *Two under par.* New York: HarperTrophy.

Hope, L. L. (1904–1979). *The Bobbsey twins* series. New York: Douglas Editions

Keene, C. (1930–current). *Nancy Drew* series. New York: Grosset & Dunlap.

Lee, H. (1960/2002). *To kill a mockingbird.* New York: Harper Perennial Classics.

London, J. (1903/2005). *Call of the wild.* New York: Pestwick House, Inc.

Martin, A. M., & Lerangris, P. (1986–2000). *The baby-sitter's club* series. New York: Scholastic Press.

McMillan, T. (1987). *Mama.* Boston: Pocket Books.

Montgomery, L. M. (1908). *Anne of green gables* series. New York: Starfire Publisher.

Park, B. (1988). *The kid in the red jacket.* New York: Random House.

Park, B. (1992–current). *Junie B. Jones* series. New York: Scholastic.

Poe, E. A. (1983). *The tell-tale heart and other writings.* New York: Bantam Classics.

Rowling, J. K. (1997–2007). *Harry Potter* series. New York: Scholastic.

Sachar, L. (1998). *Holes.* New York: Random House.

Shakespeare, W. (2004). *Taming of the shrew.* New York: Washington Square Press.

Snicket, L. (1999–2006). *Lemony Snicket's a series of unfortunate events.* New York: Harper Collins.

Staff Writers. (1999–current). *Blues clues* series. New York: Simon and Schuster.

Staff Writers. (1966–current). *Winnie the Pooh, Disney book* series. New York: Disney Press.

Stine, R. L. (1992–1997). *Goosebumps* series. New York: Scholastic Press.

Stine, R. L. (1989–1997). *Fear street* series. New York: Scholastic Press.

Tolkien, J. R. R. (1954–1955). *The lord of the rings* series. Boston, MA: Houghton Mifflin.

Wilder, L. I. (1931–1974). *Little house* series. New York: HarperCollins.

Index

About the Author

Catherine Compton-Lilly is an associate professor in Curriculum and Instruction at the University of Wisconsin–Madison. She has taught in the public school system for 18 years. She is the author of *Reading Families: The Literate Lives of Urban Children* (Teachers College Press, 2003), *Confronting Racism, Poverty and Power* (Heinemann, 2004), *Re-reading Families* (Teachers College Press, 2007), the editor of *Breaking the Silence* (International Reading Association, 2009), and co-editor of *Bedtime Stories and Book Reports* (Teachers College Press, 2010). Dr. Compton-Lilly has authored articles in the *Reading Research Quarterly, Research in the Teaching of English, The Reading Teacher, The Journal of Early Childhood Literacy, The Reading Teacher,* and *Language Arts.* Dr. Compton-Lilly engages in longitudinal research projects that last over long periods of time. In her most recent study, she followed a group of eight inner-city students from grade 1 through grade 11. Her interests include examining how time operates as a contextual factor in children's lives as they progress through school and construct their identities as students and readers.